# PRAISE FOR
## GRACEFUL DIVORCE SOLUTIONS:
### A COMPREHENSIVE AND PROACTIVE GUIDE TO SAVING YOU TIME, MONEY AND YOUR SANITY

"I got my divorce for less than the lawyer's retainer fee. Went right to mediation. It was difficult but civil. I was proud of myself. So – your book is right on the money. So here's my quote: "*Graceful Divorce Solutions* is a Godsend for divorcing couples. It will help you go through this wrenching process with your soul – and your wallet, intact." Bravo!

**- Christiane Northrup, M.D.**
Best Selling Author of *Women's Bodies, Women's Wisdom, Mother-Daughter Wisdom, and The Wisdom of Menopause*

"If you care about your well-being and the well-being of your children while going through a divorce, you need to read this book."

**- Cheryl Richardson**
Best Selling Author of *Take Time for Your Life, Stand up for Your Life, The Unmistakable Touch of Grace, and The Art of Extreme Self-Care*

"This easy-to-read guidebook, written by a seasoned attorney, provides all the basic information to help you maneuver the often treacherous path to divorce. Marcy Jones writes from the heart and gives the reader a laundry list of important suggestions that will save you from the usual escalations that often accompany divorce. For your sake, and the sake of your children, read this book and learn how you can save yourself from making disastrous mistakes."

**- Constance Ahrons, Ph.D.**
Author of *The Good Divorce and We're Still Family*

"Marcy has done a first-rate job of explaining the vital importance of choosing the right divorce process and the right professional helpers for clients who want to conserve resources, behave with civility, and keep the focus on the children. And, she helps you understand step by step how to mobilize the appropriate divorce conflict resolution process, rather than falling by default into a lawyer-driven conventional divorce that has no place for values-based joint problem solving. *Graceful Divorce Solutions* is indeed a virtual first consultation with a wise divorce counselor. It provides the information that divorcing couples need – information that they rarely will be given during a first interview with conventional divorce lawyers."

**- Pauline H. Tesler, M.A., J.D.**
Author of *Collaborative Divorce: The Revolutionary New Way to Restructure Your Family, Resolve Legal Issues, and Move on with Your Life*, and founder of the International Association of Collaborative Professionals

"This book is a must-read for anyone facing the prospect of divorce. With straightforward language and offering a clear approach, Marcy puts you back in the driver's seat so you can navigate your divorce with more power, ease and options. What you'll learn from reading this book will save you literally thousands of dollars if you went through this learning curve in a lawyer's office. In *Graceful Divorce Solutions*, Marcy essentially provides you with your first legal consultation. You learn about the different processes for divorcing, as well as the issues that you need to be thinking about. Divorce is an unfortunate reality in our society, but finding ways to reform and humanize it makes us all winners. *Graceful Divorce Solutions* offers a clear roadmap through the legal solutions, which is one of the most intimidating and daunting pieces of divorce. Whether you are going through a divorce now, thinking about separating, or wanting to support a loved one in the process, this book is an indispensible resource and will help to anchor and guide you along the way. It's a resource that has my highest recommendation."

**- Carolyn Ellis**
Author of *The 7 Pitfalls of Single Parenting: What to Avoid to Help Your Children Thrive after Divorce* and Creator of the award-winning *The Divorce Resource Kit, www.ThriveAfterDivorce.com*

"Conventional wisdom has decreed that divorce is something that is done to the participants. M. Marcy Jones, in her new book, *Graceful Divorce Solutions*, sets forth, in a clear and comprehensive manner, options for divorcing by electing from processes that allow proactive participation. This book is a great place to start your divorce education."

**- Stuart G. Webb, J.D**.
Collaborative Law Founder and Pioneer and Author of *The Collaborative Way to Divorce: The Revolutionary Method that Results in Less Stress, Lower Cost, and Happier Kids – Without Going to Court*

"Marcy takes a strong stand – this book is different, practical, and quite visionary. There is so much helpful takeaway for the reader, from the broad to the intricate – it makes the book a very helpful, almost indispensable manual. It's like an initial legal consultation, but much less inconvenient and stressful than setting up an appointment with a lawyer...not to mention much less expensive! And it will PREPARE the reader so well for that first real meeting."

**- Jill Dearman**
Part-time Prof. of Journalism, NYU, Writing Coach, Editor, and Author of *Bang the Keys: Four Steps to a Lifelong Writing Practice*

"I am thrilled to have this clear and concise resource to offer my clients who are contemplating divorce or who have decided to divorce. *Graceful Divorce Solutions* provides exactly the kind of information we all strive to share with our clients, but so often is lost in the emotional upheaval of the moment. Now our clients will have this as a reference book to use as they need and on their own time – to help them absorb this information and to keep what is really important at the forefront."

**- Lisa L. Schenkel**, **J.D.**
Collaborative Professional, Trainer, and Founding Member of Collaborative Practice Training Institute, Served as Substitute Judge in Juvenile and Domestic Relations District Courts, 28-year Family Law Attorney

"This is the definitive "go to" book to recommend to anyone, client, family or friend, who is going through a divorce or considering one. It's written by a "real" human being who experienced divorce and has years of experience as a family law attorney, so it covers the gamut. My only regret is that it wasn't in my hands years ago for the many folks I've seen who needed just this experience to inform them. The process of divorce is un-empowering for so many people. Knowledge is power, and this book will empower anyone – just to know what the divorce process will look like, how it might feel, what their choices are, and have an expert telling them that they can do this in a graceful way!"

**- Deborah M. Maxey, Ph.D.**
Licensed Professional Counselor, Licensed Marriage and
Family Therapist, Board Certified Professional Counselor,
Certified Domestic Abuse Counselor


"Marcy is a seasoned lawyer, skillful mediator and ace coach. Throughout *Graceful Divorce Solutions*, Marcy's consistently strong, constructive, and nurturing voice support the reader through all of the choices that need to be made during divorce. This book normalizes and humanizes the process and offers effective alternatives to conventional divorce. Marcy encourages taking the highest road possible, bringing your best self to the table, and moving through this time with integrity and kindness. She also helps readers be proactive—which includes finding a lawyer to partner with, rather than just blindly turning it all over to a lawyer. There's never been a more inspiring and fresh approach to divorce!"

**- Rhonda Hess**
Coaching Business Success Strategist,
Speaker, Author, and Founder of Prosperous Coach®

"*Graceful Divorce Solutions* by Marcy Jones fulfills its subtitle's promise to save you "Time, Money, and Your Sanity." As a lawyer, Marcy realized the need for people to understand their options when divorcing, and for lawyers to understand the emotional component of divorce. She thoroughly explains why the legal system should not be involved in most divorce cases—the legal system's way of turning a husband and wife against each other is not conducive to ongoing communication between the couple after divorce, and especially not beneficial to the children's welfare. Admittedly, lawyers have a bad name, but Marcy Jones has written a book that redeems many of them by showing that lawyers can care about people rather than just fighting with each other and billing their clients for their time."

- **Tyler R. Tichelaar, Ph.D.**
Author of the award-winning *Narrow Lives*

*"This book is a Godsend for divorcing couples. It will help you go through this wrenching process with your soul – and your wallet, intact."*
- Christiane Northrup, M.D.

# GRACEFUL DIVORCE SOLUTIONS

## A Comprehensive and Proactive Guide to Saving You Time, Money, and Your Sanity

AVIVA
PUBLISHING
NEW YORK

## M. MARCY JONES, J.D.
### ATTORNEY - MEDIATOR - COACH

**GRACEFUL DIVORCE SOLUTIONS:** *A Proactive and Comprehensive Guide to Saving You Time, Money, and Your Sanity*

AUTHOR'S NOTE

The material in this book is provided for informational purposes only. The reader should consult with his or her personal legal advisor before utilizing the information contained in this book. The law is different in every state. The author and the publisher assume no responsibility for any damages or losses incurred during or as a result of following this information.

Many names and identifying details of the individual examples described in this book have been changed to preserve confidentiality.

M. Marcy Jones
P. O. Box 996
Lynchburg, VA 24505
(434) 845-2463
www.GracefulDivorceSolutions.com
www.MMarcyJones.com

Library of Congress Number: 2009940472

ISBN: 978-1-935586-00-5

Published in the United States of America by Aviva Publishing

Editor: Jill Dearman

Cover & Interior Design: Fusion Creative Works, www.fusioncw.com

# DEDICATION

To my children, Collier and Jordan. You have grown into amazing adults, despite my less than stellar parenting during some tough times. Thank you for your kindness, inspiration, and constant support. I have learned so much from both of you.

And to all of you going through divorce. With my heartfelt compassion and encouragement, I hope this book will inform you, inspire you, and help you to pass through this challenging time with ease and grace.

# CONTENTS

# ACKNOWLEDGEMENTS

I am privileged and grateful to have so many wonderful people who have supported me in getting this book written and published. I deeply appreciate each and every one of them and would like to acknowledge them here.

To Sue Brundege, my coach and mentor for the nine months I was writing this book. Early in that coaching relationship I made the statement, "Someday I would like to write a book," and by the end of that coaching relationship, I had a draft of a manuscript! Your gentle guidance and support helped me to accomplish something I had only dreamed about. Thank you for showing me how to tighten up my writing and for that first round of editing. And, more importantly, thank you for your continued support in helping me to get (and keep!) the vision that I could do this.

To my editor, Jill Dearman, you are an amazingly talented writer, editor, and published author with a great sense of humor. Thank you for the excellent editing, encouragement, and helpful feedback on my writing.

To Patrick Snow, you taught me so much about publishing and helped to make this book a reality. It's one thing to do the writing. It's quite another to figure out and coordinate all the details necessary to get it from a manuscript to a published book.

To Carolyn Ellis, for your generosity in taking the time to write an amazing Foreword for me, and to everyone who wrote the wonderful endorsements that follow—Dr. Christiane Northrup, Cheryl Richardson, Pauline Tesler, Stu Web, Dr. Constance Ahrons, Jill Dearman, Dr. Deborah Maxey, Rhonda Hess, Lisa Schenkel, and Tyler Tichelaar. I am honored and humbled to have your support of this book.

And to my friends, family, and colleagues who supported me in this process, especially Melissa Wiggins, Kristen Andreae, Trula Crosier, and the rest of my "team" out there. You know who you are. You all helped me to stay the course and believe in myself. Your divine guidance and constant support has made this book a reality. You have my warmest appreciation and sincerest gratitude.

And last but certainly not least, heartfelt thanks to my former husband and my children, who have been my inspiration and greatest teachers along this journey. But for our experience, I wouldn't have had the passion, courage, or calling to write this book.

# FOREWORD
# BY CAROLYN ELLIS

Divorce is never something for which a person plans. I remember the day when I realized my own marriage—after 20 years and three children—was headed for divorce. Although I asked for the divorce, there was a voice inside my head insisting, "Hey, but this isn't supposed to happen! I thought I was going to be married happily ever after!"

As about 50% of married couples in North America discover, marriage isn't always a case of living together happily ever after. Imagine taking every significant component of your life—your most significant intimate relationship, your children, your finances, your emotional well-being, your social network, your home, your sense of identity, and sometimes even your career—and turning them all upside down all at once. Now you're getting a sense of the far-ranging scope and impact that divorce has on a person's life. This is true for both the person who chooses to leave the relationship and the one who is left behind.

Making the decision to divorce is difficult in itself. Yet charting your road through divorce and implementing this decision requires a whole level of focus and commitment that is often overlooked. Disentangling the emotional, financial, social, and romantic threads that bind people together is a monumental task. At a time in your life when your emotions are running on overdrive already, you will be asked to make fundamental decisions that will impact the rest of your life. It is a very treacherous mix because when emotions run high, intelligence typically runs low. Your need to articulate your desires clearly, advocate for the needs of yourself and your children, if you have any, and reinvent your life comes at a time when your emotional resilience will be tested to the limits.

Overlay onto this rocky emotional landscape the need to engage in the legal system. Unfortunately, the legal system and the kind of training most lawyers receive often leave much to be desired. Emotionally shell-shocked clients, with little understanding of their rights or how to create a framework for their lives after divorce, stream into lawyers' offices looking for answers. They place their power in the hands of trained legal professionals, assuming a lawyer or the court system will come up with an answer to their pain and be the vehicle for creating a plan that works and stands the test of time.

What they learn about the conventional approach of duking it out in court between two battling lawyers and a judge with an overflowing docket is that going to court is expensive, time-consuming, destructive to relationships, and extremely stressful to the entire family. Nobody really ends up a "winner" when all faith, hope, and decision-making on one's divorce is put in the hands of the attorneys. Parties often leave their court settlements dissatisfied with the outcome and with significantly less money after legal fees are paid out. Divorced parents also face the prospect of how to co-parent with each other for the next decade or two after having torpedoed the goodwill and trust needed to develop a co-parenting partnership.

At the end of the day, you must be the quarterback of the legal team. The court system and the judge view you as a file, not a family. Most lawyers are trained to view things from the adversarial lens and what's right and what's wrong. That black-and-white perspective works great if your dispute is about fulfillment of a widget contract. It doesn't work when you're talking about reframing a family system that will have an ongoing and dynamic relationship for years to come after the case is settled. What's needed is for the individual clients to direct their legal advisors in a way that elicits and executes a plan that reflects their values and supports building a new relationship. And that's where M. Marcy Jones's *Graceful Divorce Solutions* comes in.

This book is a must-read for anyone facing the prospect of divorce. With straightforward language and offering a clear approach, Marcy puts you back in the driver's seat so you can navigate your divorce with more power, ease, and options. What you'll learn from reading this book will save you literally thousands of dollars compared to if you went through this learning curve in a lawyer's office.

In this comprehensive and timely book, you'll learn why the system is broken and why it just is not set up to handle the emotional and psychological issues of divorce. A compassionate and intuitive lawyer, speaker, and advocate, Marcy has spent the last 15 years working with families going through divorce. She went to law school after her own divorce and with two young children at home, so she has been in the trenches and has studied the workings of the system from all sides. She is passionate and determined to get out her message that there are better ways of divorcing—ways that protect children and preserve relationships.

In *Graceful Divorce Solutions,* Marcy essentially provides you with your first legal consultation. You learn about the different processes for divorcing, as well as the issues that you need to be thinking about. You'll be encouraged throughout to take the highest road possible for your situation—with the understanding that there is no "one size fits all" way of going through this transition. But the important thing is you will become informed and know your options before getting caught up in the system. You will be proactive in your own case—and that is one of Marcy's primary goals throughout this book.

I am a huge advocate of ensuring information is not just enlightening on an intellectual level, but practical to implement in your daily life. *Graceful Divorce Solutions* includes not just the information you need about the legal system, but Marcy offers powerful exercises for each aspect of your divorce that will help you articulate your priorities and values on the major pieces of the divorce puzzle. This is a necessary, yet often overlooked, part of creating a divorce solution that works not just legally, but emotionally, over the long haul. So get your pens and notebooks ready and decide for yourself that you will take an active and informed role in this journey upon which you are about to embark.

Throughout this book, Marcy advocates change—change in the legal system, change in the way lawyers represent clients, and change in the way clients come to the table. Here she has given you the information and encouragement you need to be able to partner with your lawyer or mediator or collaborative professional. This book is an invaluable tool to set you up for a better divorce experience.

I firmly believe you don't have to settle simply for surviving your divorce, as many people assume. Instead, I believe divorce offers huge lessons for us and that it's possible to thrive after divorce. As a coach and trainer, I've shared this message with thousands of people from around the world.

Divorce is an unfortunate reality in our society, but finding ways to reform and humanize it makes us all winners. M. Marcy Jones's *Graceful Divorce Solutions* offers a clear roadmap through the legal solutions, which is one of the most intimidating and daunting pieces of divorce. Whether you are going through a divorce now, thinking about separating, or wanting to support a loved one in the process, this book is an indispensable resource and will help to anchor and guide you along the way. It's a resource that has my highest recommendation!

**Carolyn Ellis**

Author of *The 7 Pitfalls of Single Parenting: What to Avoid to Help Your Children Thrive after Divorce* and Creator of the award-winning *The Divorce Resource Kit*
www.ThriveAfterDivorce.com

# INTRODUCTION

The ideas in this book have been in my head for years. After experiencing my own divorce and then going to law school and practicing family law, I knew there was a need for change in the way people *do* divorce. The old adage, "If it ain't broke, don't fix it," does not apply here. The system *is* broken when it comes to resolving family issues. Either that, or we are all participating in a form of collective insanity! The conventional way of divorcing is just crazy—it's destructive to families and unnecessarily expensive. It's time to stop this insanity and take action to implement change.

Right now we don't *do* divorce, it *does* us. Simply stated, the whole system is illogical and out of control. By using our common sense and a bit of emotional intelligence, we can begin to apply some practical solutions that are needed in order to protect the many families and children who are affected by this life transition.

My own divorce wasn't as bad as some you hear about, but it was still difficult emotionally and financially. For most people going through a divorce, there is a period of what I call "personal insanity." That's the cycle that feels like a wild and crazy roller coaster ride, where one minute you think the ride is over and you're ready to get off, and you've just about caught your breath, and the next minute you're back in the loops and curves, screaming your lungs out.

I wasn't prepared for that roller coaster ride, and I wasn't very good at protecting my children from my personal insanity during all the chaos. To this day, I have regrets about the way I handled myself at times. My intention was always to put my children's needs first, but that didn't always happen. I did it better some times than others. If I'd known then what I know now, I would have done it better, and my children would have been spared some of my ups and downs. I hope this information will help you to do it better. If you can at least recognize that it is a crazy time, then you can be intentional about when and how you choose to release and act upon those crazy feelings. Ideally, you will save it for when the children are not around.

As I write this, I'm reminded of the first time I tried to quit smoking after smoking for fifteen years. What a shocking experience! Like the roller coaster ride of divorce, I was not prepared for how hard it would be. I had not informed myself about what to expect. I thought I could just get up one day and decide not to smoke. Boy, was I wrong. It didn't work that way. I felt like I'd lost my best friend. I thought I was going crazy. I cried. After a few days, I gave up. If you've ever tried to break an addiction, I'm sure you can relate to this.

Soon after I educated myself about what to expect and I made a plan, I was eventually able to succeed. It was still hard, but I was able to do it because I knew what to expect and had a plan to follow when things got tough. It's the same idea here. Informing yourself about the process and your choices and making a plan for yourself will help you do it better. It will likely still be hard, but nothing compared to the experience of moving forward blindly.

Following my separation and divorce, I found myself in the same situation as many divorced women. My standard of living took a dive and I needed to make more money. I had been home with my children until they started school and had worked only part-time. I had taught high school, but I didn't want to go back to teaching. So I began to look at graduate school programs. I wanted to do something that would allow me to make a decent income so I could support my children and myself and that would also give me the freedom I needed to be available to them.

For some reason, law school seemed to be a fit for what I was looking for. That in itself was amazing to me, because I had worked for lawyers, had been married to a lawyer, and had even been known to say, "I would never want to *be* a lawyer!" But there was a voice in my head that kept pushing me to check it out. I thought that maybe if I were a lawyer, I could help people through their divorces in a more graceful and positive way, and perhaps doing this would even heal some of my wounds.

I perceived a huge need for compassionate and psychologically savvy lawyers to help people deal with the unpredictability and emotional intensity of the divorce process. So that's what I did. I applied to one school only. I figured if I got in, then it was meant to be. If not, then I needed to move on to something else.

I was accepted and started law school at the age of 37, with two young children at home, ages 10 and 7. Once I started taking family law classes, I knew this was the area I was drawn to. Family law was a critical area where change was needed, and also where I felt I could make a difference. After reading case after case, it was profoundly clear that "the law" did not address the real needs of families when they were in crisis, whether it was divorce, custody, support, domestic violence, or parental termination. It was also profoundly clear that the legal system simply was not designed to deal with the intensely emotional and psychological issues of families in crisis. I knew there had to be a better way.

This book has emerged from my own journey of intense frustration with the legal system and with lawyers in general. A few years ago, I almost left my law practice. I was disillusioned and disgusted with the legal system, the way people divorced, and the way many lawyers made the process worse. I knew there were better ways, but I felt powerless to effect any significant change in the process.

When people are used to doing things a certain way for a long time, change is difficult. Lawyers are no different. And when people going to lawyers don't have the right information to help them make the best choices for themselves, they tend to give over control of their cases to the lawyers and ultimately give up their power of choice. This happens especially as cases escalate and take on a life of their own.

What happens is that the clients have no idea what's going on—they can't be part of the process because they don't know how to—they don't know what they don't know, so they don't know they actually have choices, or what other information they need, or who to ask, or even what to ask. They feel lost, powerless, and fearful of the unknown, so they look to lawyers or the legal system for guidance. And many lawyers are happy to oblige. After all, this is what they were trained to do.

And this is often where the trouble starts. Because of the client's lack of information and understanding, the lawyer is likely to take over the case and proceed in a way that may be adverse to what the client really wants. I don't necessarily believe this happens on a conscious level, but rather, it is because of the lack of understanding, communication, and planning on the part of both lawyers and their clients. It's an unfortunate combination of clients not having an understanding about their choices and their ability to be actively involved in their own divorces and of lawyers not having an understanding of the emotional and psychological component of the divorcing process.

Additionally, when one client and one lawyer want to play nice, but the spouse and the other lawyer want to fuss and fight, it becomes difficult to keep a case from getting out of control. I've seen this happen in case after case. I've seen families torn apart by our adversarial system, and it makes my stomach hurt. I knew it didn't have to be that way, but I just didn't know what I, as one lawyer, could do about it. The answer that kept coming to me was two-fold:

- **first, change the way lawyers think about and handle divorces**

- **second, get honest, reliable information to the clients about their options so they can be actively involved in their own divorce process**

The question for me was how to do this. What role could I play in helping lawyers and clients see the necessity of making these important shifts?

Although I was familiar with mediation and saw the mediation process as a better way to go through divorce, it wasn't being used much where I lived. And, of course, it wasn't for everybody either. Then, in 2003, I heard about a process called collaborative practice, and I knew that, finally, here was a process that was respectful, forward-looking, and met the needs of the whole family. It was brilliant and made perfect sense to me.

This process allowed each spouse to have his or her own lawyer, and therefore have his or her own advocate and advisor, but the clincher was that the couple agreed from the outset *not* to go to court. When the threat of "going to court" is taken out of the picture, it changes the whole dynamic. Settlement is the goal from the beginning of the case, not at the end on the courthouse steps, after all the damage has been done. I could see how this process would allow parents to maintain a decent relationship so they could still be good co-parents to their children, even though they were divorced. This was really a great motivation for me. I wanted to be part of protecting the children.

When I went to the senior partner at the firm I was in at the time to ask whether I could go to a two-day basic training in collaborative practice, he looked at the information and responded, "This isn't practicing law." In his mind, if you weren't preparing to go to court, you weren't practicing law. If you weren't preparing for court, then you must be *afraid* to go to court and fight the fight, which is, after all, what lawyers are trained to do! It's called "zealous advocacy," and is, unfortunately, the thought process I believe has contributed to making divorces much more adversarial than they should be or need to be. This is still a very common reaction among lawyers who have practiced for many years. They just don't see how this process can work, or how it fits in with the lawyer image.

Learning about collaborative practice gave me new hope for the legal profession and for my own law practice. I was determined to get this training and to spread the word about collaborative practice. Fortunately, other lawyers in my community also saw the value in this new way of helping people to divorce. The truth is, most lawyers who specialize in family law have seen the destructiveness of the conventional divorce process and are looking for a better way. They are stressed out and burned out from dealing with people's intense personal issues and emotions and the insanity of the legal system.

Collaborative divorce was the answer.

I trained in collaborative practice, along with several other local lawyers. Soon we had clients who saw the value in this process and were excited to have this option. These cases were so successful and positive, we were ecstatic. The contrast between this process and the traditional process was unbelievable. When one of my first cases was completed, both clients hugged both lawyers; I assure you, you are not likely to see this happen when clients walk out of the courtroom after litigation.

The challenge now was to get the word out to people and enroll them in the collaborative process. The problem was that often one party would want to collaborate but the other wouldn't. Or more likely, the other just didn't know about this as an option. At the point where papers were filed and an adversarial action was begun, the case would inevitably escalate. The spouse who wanted to collaborate now needed to respond similarly just for protection. That's just the way the system works. One person cannot collaborate alone. It takes two people willing to come to the table and take the higher road.

Our challenge was to get our own clients to see the value in the collaborative process, and then to get information to their spouses about collaborative divorce *before their spouses* hired litigation lawyers.

When I became frustrated with how long it was taking to get lawyers on board to support this process, I decided to get the word out in a bigger way. When I looked at the books on the market about divorce, I saw a real need for a guide like this—straightforward, easy to read, no legalese, and filled with exactly the valuable information people need when thinking about separating or divorcing.

**This book is your manual, the first place to go, to get the nuts and bolts information you need before you begin your journey.**

My vision is that more and more people thinking about divorce or going through divorce seek out the collaborative professional or mediation/settlement expert rather than the litigation lawyer. My intention is that the information provided here will teach, motivate, and inspire you to make the best and most informed choices for you and your family and will help you to take the highest road possible under your circumstances.

Do you have children? If so, even though this is your divorce and you are going through a difficult time, it isn't just about you. It's also about your children. The decisions you make now will make a huge difference in how your life looks down the road. They will also make a huge difference in your children's lives.

And if you don't have children, the decisions you make now about the process you use for divorcing will also make a huge difference for you and your spouse in how the rest of your life goes. With or without children, your emotional and financial lives are impacted in different ways depending on the process used.

None of this is easy. I get that, from personal experience and the experiences of many clients. But it can be done in a better way, a more graceful way, and one that costs you less money, less time, and causes you less stress. Even if you aren't able to keep your divorce from becoming adversarial, the information in this book will be of tremendous value to you. It will raise your awareness about what to be thinking about and give you ideas about reaching resolutions you may not have otherwise considered or even known were available.

I object to the conventional divorce process, and so should you! Just as people have become more proactive about their health care and their interactions with their physicians, the time has come for people to be more proactive regarding their legal issues and their interactions with their lawyers. If you're reading this book, I assume you're looking for information and answers to your burning questions.

The information here will give you the foundation you need to begin the process of figuring out what's best for you and your family. Once you are aware of this important information, then you can be intentional and deliberate in your choices. And that's the whole point—get informed, know your options, make your choices, and find the best professionals to help you carry out your plan.

Your mission is to be involved in your process, to partner with experienced professionals who can help you, and to keep your case moving in the direction you want. This is your ultimate goal, and this book is designed to help you achieve that goal.

Good Luck!

# 1

# GETTING DIVORCED?
## IT'S TIME FOR CHANGE

What do *you* think of when you think of divorce? For most people, the words that come to mind are—ugly, unpleasant, expensive, stressful, scary, emotional, painful, etc. By changing the way we *think* about divorce, we will change the way we *do* divorce—and we will do it better.

Why does this matter? Divorce impacts our society in many ways. The negative consequences of divorce are well known and documented. I have to believe that if people knew better, they would do better. I have to believe people would not do the things I've seen them do to each other, to their children, and in the presence of their children if they truly understood the long-term damaging effects of their behavior.

One of the problems is that our legal system provides a legal solution to something that is only partially a legal problem.

Ending a marriage is a complicated process. The legal piece is the easy part. Dealing with the emotional, financial and social ramifications are the bigger pieces. Recognizing this truth is the first step. We will change the way we do divorce when we change the way we think about divorce and realize there is a great deal more involved than getting the judge's signature on a final divorce decree.

Raising people's awareness will also raise their consciousness, and this means that change can happen because they will no longer buy into the current system. They will understand the value of doing it differently. And then the legal system will just be a *piece* of the process, rather than the driving force.

Statistics show that half of all first marriages end in divorce. That's 50%. If it's not you, it's someone you know. Isn't it time we figure out how to stop waging divorce wars and find ways to end marriages more peacefully? Think about the difference just this thought process could make!

We cringe when we hear that someone we know is separated and divorcing. We think, "Poor thing," or "Sure glad it isn't me!" It's like the person has just been diagnosed with a terminal illness. As a whole, we are about as comfortable talking about divorce as we are talking about illness or dying. This avoidance of openly discussing divorce topics needs to change. The fact that people aren't comfortable talking about divorce (or are embarrassed by their personal situations) keeps them from getting the information they need.

Fortunately, a change is already underway across the United States and the world. People are hearing more about mediation and collaborative divorce options. As positive as this is, the change has been excruciatingly slow. Yet, with the current state of the economy, I believe people are seeking out more efficient and cheaper ways to divorce. Prolonged court battles are a luxury few can afford anymore.

One important key to make this change happen more quickly is for people to become familiar with this information BEFORE they seek out legal representation. Unfortunately, too many lawyers benefit from the status quo of divorce. If you're motivated to change the status quo, and you want to be part of the change, you need information to make that happen. The information in this book will enable you to be proactive about your own situation and make your own process better.

Here's how:

- **You'll learn about your process choices (ways of divorcing) in an easy, non-threatening, and non-intimidating way, so you can make the best decisions for you from an informed place.**

- **When you make conscious decisions about how you'll go through your divorce, you're able to maintain more control of your case and work more effectively with your lawyer and the system, which is infinitely better** than not doing this and having your case spiral out of control and not understanding what's happening.

- The information in this book will give you confidence and encouragement and will eliminate that "fear of the unknown" that can be so paralyzing.

- You'll learn the value and importance of taking the time to get the Big Picture of your situation (how you want your life to look when your divorce is over) and then, through reverse engineering, you'll strategize how to achieve that reality for yourself and your family, going from where you are now to where you want to be.

- You'll learn the value of the collaborative approach to resolving conflict and how this skill, which involves active listening and good communicating, can be incorporated into every area of your life.

- If you have children, you'll learn how they may be affected by your divorce, as well as the steps you can take to minimize the impact on them.

Does this sound too good to be true? It's not. It's simply a matter of becoming informed, looking before you leap, and making the best plan for you and your family. Because divorce is such an emotional event, too often people just stumble blindly through it. They don't think through the actions they are taking. The truth is that when you're going through this major life transition, it's often difficult to think at all. That's why people end up in such messy divorce situations—because they haven't been able to act apart from their emotions and to be intentional enough about what they want.

**Consider the rest of this book as your first legal consultation**. It's a lot cheaper than the real one and will set you up to think carefully through your options so you can make better decisions and have a more successful divorce experience.

At the end of each chapter, I will ask you questions about your own situation. Get a notebook or journal ready and work through these questions as you go through the book. Answer each question as thoroughly and in as much detail as possible. This is important because it will help you to clarify your own feelings and beliefs, and also to have a better understanding of your own situation. You are likely to gain insights from writing out your answers that you won't get from just sitting and thinking about them.

What's going to help you the most is to have a clear, honest picture of where you are right now, to have a clear understanding of your options right now, and then to begin to formulate a plan to get you from where you are to where you want to go. Having a clear vision of your choices and then of how you want to go through your process will make a tremendous difference in your experience.

**Here's the Nutshell Version in three steps of how you can change the conventional approach to divorcing and do it better. The rest of this book will show you the way:**

1. Decide what you want your life to look like a year from now and then five years from now. I call this the Big Picture view.

2. Become informed about your process choices and how they work, and decide which one is best for your situation and circumstances.

3. Choose the most skilled professionals who can advise and support you through the process you choose and help you achieve your overall goals.

And now, read on to learn about the specific problems and challenges with the way we currently do divorce and about some new and innovative ways of divorcing and resolving conflict which will make a difference in your life and make the world a better place.

# 2

# DEFINING THE PROBLEM: THE WAY WE DO DIVORCE

In the legal world, dissolving a marriage is not unlike dissolving a business partnership. There are assets and debts to be divided. However, in a marriage there are also emotional and psychological issues that need to be addressed. And then there are the children.

Here's the problem: our court system was developed in England over the last 500 years and involves a process primarily designed to deal with the resolution of one time issues between people who are typically not related and who are not likely to have any ongoing contact. Does that sound like any family you know? Historically, the courts have dealt mostly with criminal, property, and financial issues. It's only been in the last 30 years or so that there has been a surge of family law cases in the court system.

The trouble is that family law is different. The courts were never designed to resolve cases involving custody and visitation of children. These are seldom, if ever, one time cases, and these cases involve people who are related and will most likely have an ongoing relationship. What that ongoing relationship will look like is the key. The current legal system sets people up to be adversarial, when in truth we have a family that may look different after the divorce, but which, nevertheless, is still a family. When you have to be adversarial with people with whom you're supposed to have an ongoing relationship, well, what kind of sense does that make?

So when a divorce is final and there are children involved, don't Moms and Dads still need to be able to talk to each other? Don't children still need to know that Mom and Dad are both there for them and will support them, regardless of where they live? And if there aren't children involved, don't most husbands and wives still want to be decent toward each other?

In the conventional divorce model, people operate under a huge misconception that "going to court" will solve their problems or that a judge will hear their side and rule in their favor. They believe that justice will be served if the judge can just hear their side. Although this does happen occasionally, most often the clients walk out of court feeling frustrated, let down, and misunderstood.

So what are the downsides to the conventional divorce model? It's expensive, time-consuming, stressful, and destructive to family relationships. Let's discuss each one of these in more detail.

**Divorce is expensive.** Depending on where you live and the size of your marital estate, the cost of the conventional divorce can be anywhere from a few thousand dollars to hundreds of thousands of dollars. Typically, you will meet with your attorney, sign a retainer agreement, and pay a retainer fee. This money goes into the lawyer's trust account and is drawn out as he or she works on your case. The lawyer's hourly rate varies with locality and experience, ranging from $100 an hour to $1,000 an hour. The typical hourly range is $200 to $500. The lawyer keeps track of his time and bills you at his or her hourly rate.

If there are disagreements as to values of assets, you are also likely to have expert witness fees for home appraisals and business evaluations. It gets pricey to hire an expert to do an appraisal or an evaluation and then to bring that person to court to testify on your behalf. This can add thousands of dollars to your costs.

The picture you may have in your head of lawyers sitting in their offices and tediously going through your financial information is accurate. It's their job to know all the ins and outs of your situation and to prepare exhibits and documents for trial to put you in the best light before the judge. It's their job to "get you the best deal." And they will bill you for every minute of their time spent to get you that deal.

You can see how quickly the costs of a divorce can add up. This reality is something a lot of people don't really get when they start the divorce process, and unfortunately, something lawyers aren't always clear about explaining. Also, what appears to be a fairly straightforward case at first may become more complicated as the case progresses and as the lawyer finds out more information, adding time and cost to the divorce.

**Divorce is time-consuming.** From filing a divorce to the final order, a conventional divorce can take from one to three years if the case is contested. Once the case is finished, there is also the possibility of appeal if one side or the other doesn't like the ruling of the court. It can take up to a year to get your divorce case into court. Then you can show up for court on your scheduled day, only to find your case continued (delayed) for any number of reasons—someone is sick, a witness isn't available, reports weren't submitted in time, the case ahead of yours didn't finish in time, etc.

These are but a few of the factors that contribute to a case being continued, usually resulting in several months delay before getting back into court. The most common thing I hear from my clients is, "I just want it over now!" If that describes you, then the legal system is not your friend. There is nothing quick or efficient about the conventional divorce process. Court dockets can be frustratingly unpredictable.

**Divorce is stressful.** When people don't know what to expect, they become anxious and stressed. And with legal professionals speaking what seems like a foreign language, most people don't know what to expect. The fear of the unknown can have a paralyzing and debilitating effect on people (in other words, it makes them nuts!).

People are anxious and stressed because their future is completely up in the air. There is no certainty about anything. Here are the most common questions people have:

- What will happen when we go to court?

- Where will the children live?

- How will I afford to live?

- Will I have to move?

- What will my spouse say about me on the witness stand?

- What will the judge think?

All they know is what their lawyer tells them, but lawyers cannot predict the future. They can explain how the case will proceed once you walk into the courtroom, but they can't answer these other questions. The judge will answer those questions. So people turn their lives over to their lawyers and judges and put their trust in them. Sometimes this works well, but more often it doesn't.

In addition to facing the unexpected and unknown, the expense incurred and time involved to reach a resolution also contribute to the stress. During the time spent waiting to go to court, there is typically an escalation of emotions, especially as the clients realize the financial cost of the process and that they are powerless over the pace of the process. This is hard on the spouses, who feel like their entire lives are in limbo. If there are children, it can be even harder on them. They often feel pulled between Mom and Dad, wanting to please both and not hurt either's feelings. They are caught in the middle, not a place where they should be. The longer it takes to reach resolution, the more difficult it is for everyone involved.

**Divorce destroys family relationships.** Finally, the conventional divorce model often destroys family relationships. It's difficult to co-parent children after trying to annihilate your spouse, whether in negotiation proceedings or in the courtroom. When your goal is to make your spouse look as bad as possible—so you can get custody, more time with the children, or more of the marital estate—a lot gets said, true and untrue. It's difficult to recover from this and to have the kind of trusting relationship necessary to effectively co-parent children. Hurt feelings from harmful statements often lead to retaliation and bad behavior. Escalation is common and seems to take on a life of its own.

When spouses fight and go to court, other family relationships are harmed as well. Siblings, in-laws, and other close family members on both sides get dragged into the fray. It's difficult to recover from this and maintain these relationships after the divorce is over, especially if the children have suffered throughout the process.

So there is the gloom and doom report of conventional divorce. Wouldn't it make sense to *start* your case from a place of settlement? The usual theme (or threat!) is "I'll try to negotiate with you, but if you don't agree with what I want, then we'll just go to court and let the judge decide." Imagine how a shift in thinking from the beginning would change the way your divorce plays out by:

- encouraging mutual respect between you and your spouse

- allowing you to control the process rather than the court system

- saving you and your spouse time, money, and undue emotional turmoil, and

- emphasizing the needs of your children

This is what I emphasize to my clients from the first phone call and the first consultation. We need to do divorce better, by becoming more aware of our choices and more proactive in our decision-making from the beginning. How? Keep reading. But first, get out your notebook and answer these questions. Remember to answer with as much detail as possible.

And since some folks don't like to write in books, and since it's vitally important to this process that you take some time to think about and write out your responses to the following questions, I have provided a blank template of this for you. Visit my website at www.GracefulDivorceSolutions.com/book to download your copy. No excuses now for not doing these exercises!

## ASK YOURSELF:

What is MY experience of divorce?

_____

_____

_____

_____

Is it my own experience, meaning my parents were divorced or I've been divorced before? Or do I know about divorce from friends or other family members? What is it that I know, or think I know, about divorce from these experiences?

_____

_____

_____

_____

What is my belief about divorce? Do I believe that divorce is always a terrible thing? Is it true that it's always a terrible thing?

_____

_____

_____

_____

Do I know any couples who have done it well?

_____

_____

_____

_____

What did they do differently from the ones I know who had a terrible ugly divorce?

_____

_____

_____

What effect do these ideas have on the way I think about divorce?

_____

_____

_____

Fill in the blanks: (Don't think on these too long – just write whatever comes to your mind, whether it makes sense to you or not, just write it down here.)

When I think about divorce, I think of

_____

_____

_____

My biggest fear about divorce is

_____

_____

_____

The best scenario I can imagine for my situation is

_____

_____

_____

(Describe very specifically how you want your divorce to go.)

# 3

# WHAT'S YOUR STORY?
# WHERE ARE YOU NOW?

When I have a consultation with a new client, I first find out his or her story. I ask a few questions and let the person talk. To know how to move forward and make decisions, it's important to understand where my client has been.

Every case is different. People need to understand their own individual situations, how they got there, and where they want to go. Then they can learn about their process choices so they can each pick the best one for their individual situations.

Here are some of the important questions I ask and why I am interested in this information:

**How long have you been married?** The length of your marriage is primarily important with regard to division of your assets and debts and the payment of spousal support. Courts will look at whether the marriage is short-term, meaning just a few years, or long-term, meaning 15 to 20 years or more. Short-term marriages are easiest to resolve as there are fewer assets and the parties will usually just take what they brought into the marriage and go their separate ways. The longer the marriage, the more complicated these issues become.

**How old are you? How old is your spouse?** The answers to these questions could impact the payment of spousal support and division of property. For example, if the parties are in their 50's and the wife has been a homemaker throughout most of the marriage and out of the workforce for 25 years, and the husband is a well-paid executive, then the wife will need to receive spousal support in order to pay her living expenses. Likewise, if the parties are in their 50's and the wife's income is greater than the husband's, and it's unlikely he would be able to make enough to meet his monthly living expenses, then the wife may end up paying spousal support to the husband. If the parties are younger and/or are equally capable of financially supporting themselves, then spousal support is not likely to be an issue at all.

**What is the physical, mental, and emotional condition of each of you?** The answer to this question will also impact how the property is divided and the payment of support. If there are issues of mental illness, the case will need to be handled somewhat differently in order to insure that the person with the mental illness is properly advised and represented throughout the process. If there isn't a diagnosed mental illness, but there are other mental health issues, then that too will affect how the case goes and is important information to have. I address this issue again in Chapter Seven about the Four Divorces, as well as Chapter Eleven.

**How much education does each one of you have?** Again, the answer to this question will affect how your case goes. There is a big difference in a case where both parties are equally educated and the case where one has a GED and the spouse has a Ph.D. This information will impact the division of property and the payment of support.

**How many times has each one of you been married?** This information is helpful in knowing the previous experiences of the clients, which may be affecting how they are dealing with the current situation. Often people have certain beliefs based on past experiences which need to be debunked in order for them to be able to take a different path and have a different mindset about their current situation.

**How many children do you have? What are their names and ages?** This helps to put the family picture into perspective and to be able to anticipate the issues that will need to be addressed and resolved.

**Do your children have any special needs?** If so, this can affect the decisions made regarding custody, visitation, and child support. For example, I had a case where the couple had two children, both of whom were autistic. The mother was with the children the majority of the time, working with them herself and working with the schools to make sure they were getting all the services possible to help them. Since these children needed stability and consistency in order to thrive, this was a case where the children needed to live primarily with the mother and not have frequent changes in their schedule. Also, the mother was limited in terms of employment since she needed to be there for the children except for a few hours when they were in school, and this had an impact on the amount of child support and spousal support the father was ordered to pay.

**What is your employment status and income? And what is your spouse's employment status and income?** Obviously there will be a difference in a case where both parties are employed and making approximately equal incomes, and cases where both are employed but one spouse is making significantly more than the other, and then the cases where one spouse is employed and the other is not. A factor to be considered here will be the decisions the parties made regarding employment. For example, if they mutually decided that one of the parents would stay home with the children because they felt that was best for their children, and that parent has been out of the workforce throughout the marriage, the fact that they made that decision together is important in determining future support.

**How is money managed in your home? How are bills paid and by whom?** I have often been amazed to find how one spouse has managed the money and paid all the bills throughout the marriage and the other is practically clueless as to how much money they have or earn or what their bills are. I've had both husbands and wives as clients in the position of being the spouse with no information about the family finances. In that case, it's important that this person become informed and proactive and especially that he or she learns to take control of his or her own finances in the future.

**Are your bank accounts joint or separate?** If the spouses have joint accounts and are separated or plan to separate, it's smart to begin the process of setting up separate accounts and dividing their monthly income and obligations.

**What do you own and how is your property titled, i.e., houses, cars, bank accounts? How much equity is in your home, vehicles, or other property? Do you and/or your spouse have retirement accounts? How much credit card debt do you have? Are they joint or separate obligations?** These questions are important to help determine your assets and debts. You'll find more specific information on this in Chapter Twelve, but for now, just know that marital property is anything acquired during the marriage, with marital funds, from the date you were married until the date you separated. It doesn't matter who paid for it. If either you or your spouse purchased it during the marriage, then it's marital. Separate property is anything you or your spouse owned prior to the marriage, anything given as a gift to either of you by someone other than your spouse, or anything inherited by either of you that has been kept separate. So equity that has accrued in your home through the course of your marriage is marital. Value that has accrued in a 401(k) retirement plan during the course of the marriage is marital. Likewise, debt that has accrued during the marriage for the benefit of the family is also marital. Now you can see how ending a marriage is like ending a business. The first step is to determine the assets and the debts, and the next step is to figure out how to divide them between you and your spouse.

This information is important to get a picture of your current situation. Go through these questions now and write down your answers. This is good preparation for you as we proceed.

Once I have a picture of the family, I then ask some questions about what happened in the marriage. I want to hear about why you came to see me. What caused you to pick up the phone and schedule an appointment? I also ask questions to determine how you communicate with each other, what you think is going on with your spouse, how your children are doing, and what you think needs to happen from this time forward. It's at this point that we talk about what's important to you and how you want your life to look when the divorce is done.

But first, make sure you have written out answers to the general questions above. Additionally, write down your answers to the following questions. These are designed to help give you a clear and honest picture of your current situation:

(Again, if you are one who doesn't like to write in books, and since it's vitally important to this process that you take some time to think about and write out your responses to the following questions, I have provided a blank template of this for you at my website. Visit www.GracefulDivorceSolutions.com/book to download your copy. No excuses now for not doing these exercises!)

### *ASK YOURSELF:*

What happened in my marriage to bring me to where I am right now?

_____

_____

_____

_____

In looking back from where I am now, were there red flags? What were they? Are there signs I missed that now seem obvious? Could I have seen this coming?

_____

_____

_____

_____

How have I tried to make things work up until now?

_____

_____

_____

_____

_____

Have I considered other options to divorcing, like counseling or reconciliation, or have I made a firm decision that I'm ready to divorce?

_____

_____

_____

_____

_____

Have I sought help from anyone, like a minister, rabbi, or counselor?

_____

_____

_____

_____

_____

If so, what have I learned from this person or experience?

_____

_____

_____

_____

_____

How do my spouse and I communicate with each other?

_____

_____

_____

_____

_____

What do I think is going on with my spouse right now?

_____

_____

_____

_____

_____

How are my children doing right now?

_____

_____

_____

_____

# 4

# WHAT'S IMPORTANT TO YOU AND WHERE DO YOU WANT TO BE?

We've talked about the limitations of the conventional divorce process and how the legal system is simply not set up to deal with family and relationship conflicts. You've spent time writing about your own experiences and beliefs about divorce, and I challenged you to begin thinking about divorce differently.

Next we looked at your situation, and I asked you to write out your story very specifically. What exactly is going on in your life right now and what has brought you to this point? There is great value in going through this process of thinking about your situation and writing it out. Sometimes we gain amazing insights when we are quiet for a few minutes and put pen to paper. Acknowledging where we are and how we got there helps to clear the path for where we want to go.

In this chapter, I want you to think about what's important to you. And by this I mean what's really, really, really important? Go to a quiet place with your journal. Get comfortable, grab some tea or coffee, and carefully consider the following questions. As difficult as it may be for you right now, do everything within your power to answer these questions from your highest and best self and not from the place of emotional pain and present fear. You can do it. It's called getting the **Big Picture** for your life. Remember, the more detail you can get down on paper, the better.

- **What do you want your life to look like when your divorce is over?**

- **What kind of relationship do you want with your spouse when it's over?**

- **If you have children, what kind of relationship do you want them to have with each of you when it's over?**

- **What kind of experience do you want this to be for you? How do you want to feel as you go through your divorce?**

- **How do you want your children to remember the experience of your divorce?**

These are challenging questions.

Do most people ask themselves these questions when thinking about a divorce or actually beginning the divorce process? Do you think the conventional divorce process take these questions into consideration? Unfortunately, no. Most people enter into the divorce process without much information and without considering the outcome of their actions.

**IF YOU GET ONLY ONE THING FROM THIS BOOK, GET THIS—HOW YOU ANSWER THESE QUESTIONS WILL CHANGE THE WAY YOUR DIVORCE GOES. AND CHANGING THE WAY YOUR DIVORCE GOES WILL CHANGE THE WAY THE REST OF YOUR LIFE GOES.**

But it starts with you, the person in the midst of the crisis. At a time when it's the most difficult for you to think clearly and to make good decisions, you *must*. You must do whatever it takes to focus and consider what is important to you and your family. If you can see the Big Picture for yourself, meaning you are very clear about what you want your life to look like down the road, then you can change the way you *do* divorce. The benefit to you and your family is immeasurable.

If you have children, start by thinking about them. According to psychologists, when parents are divorcing, their children do best when:

1. They continue to have frequent contact with both parents;

2. They see their parents cooperate and be civil with each other; and

3. Their lives remain as much the same as possible.

It's important for children that their parents communicate with each other about them so their lives continue with as little change as possible. Like you, your children need time to adjust to the divorce. They don't need all areas of their lives to be in transition at the same time.

By deciding now that you want to have a good relationship with your spouse after your divorce, even if it is just for the children's sake, then the decisions you make now about the divorce process can make that a reality. I'm not saying this is easy. What I am saying is that it can be done if you make that decision and then get the help you need to support you along the way. This is called being "proactive."

Whether you have children or not, going through your divorce without first deciding what you want your post-divorce life to look like, is like getting in a car with no knowledge of how to drive and then heading the wrong way down a one way street. It's highly unlikely that scenario will turn out well. And it's just as unlikely your divorce will turn out well if you don't plan ahead.

Another benefit to deciding now what you want your life to look like is that you can also preserve other important family relationships. When people disagree and go to court, all members of your family are affected, not just you and your children. It's difficult for in-laws and others to recover when harsh words are said. However, if you can reach a peaceful resolution, you and your children have the benefit of maintaining better relationships with extended family members. Everyone wins.

Getting the Big Picture *first* gives you a goal to work toward and keeps you on track so you can act with integrity throughout the process and can more readily reach a fair and acceptable settlement. Again, this doesn't mean it will be easy for you. What it means is that by making a conscious and thoughtful plan about your post-divorce life, you will ease your way through the process with integrity, dignity, and grace. It may not look or feel like this at the time, but if you hold fast to your intentions and your plan, this will be the end result.

The question I ask so many of my clients is this: Is it more important to get your "pound of flesh," or is it more important for you to be a healthy, balanced person and parent? I can tell you from my experience that getting that "pound of flesh," results in little satisfaction. Likely, you will still be angry, and that anger can permeate every area of your life.

So, what do you want? I don't care what your partner did or didn't do. I care about who you are and what you want. I care about getting you through this process as gracefully as possible. I care about helping you to set up the best post-divorce life possible. Despite what you may think or feel right now, divorce doesn't have to be the end of the world, and it doesn't have to be the worst thing that happens to you. It doesn't have to define who you are.

Right now, it's time for you to focus on yourself and what you need to do to thrive under your circumstances. If you have children, then you also need to focus on their needs. This is the most positive and productive way to expend your energy.

This mindset will serve you well as you move through this experience.

Review the questions again for this chapter and answer them as thoughtfully and with as much detail as possible. Focusing on these details will help you stay the course you choose.

(Again, if you are one who doesn't like to write in books, and since it's vitally important to this process that you take some time to think about and write out your responses to the following questions, I have provided a blank template of this for you at my website. Visit www.GracefulDivorceSolutions.com/book to download your copy. No excuses now for not doing these exercises!)

### *ASK YOURSELF:*

What's important to me? (get below the surface on this one and write out what is really, really important to you)

_____

_____

_____

_____

What do I want my life to look like when my divorce is over?

_____

_____

_____

_____

What kind of relationship do I want with my spouse when it's over?

_____

_____

_____

_____

What kind of relationship do I want my children to have with each of us when it's over?

_____

_____

_____

_____

What kind of experience do I want this to be for me?

_____

_____

_____

_____

How do I want to feel as I go through my divorce?

_____

_____

_____

_____

How do I want my children to remember the experience of this divorce?

_____

_____

_____

_____

# 5

# THE TRUTH ABOUT
# CHILDREN AND DIVORCE

In this chapter, I want to focus specifically on how you can best help your children throughout this process. If you don't have children, feel free to skip ahead to the next chapter.

It's especially important to the well-being of your children that you and your spouse find ways to deal with your conflict without becoming enmeshed in a legal battle. I cannot emphasize this point strongly enough. Your children's present and future emotional health is at stake. As difficult as it may be when you are going through this tumultuous time yourself, you have to focus on what's best for your children. Study after study shows that children do best when their parents are able to set aside their disagreements (at least in their presence) and focus on what's best for them.

**The truth about children and divorce is that children do well when both parents remain committed to their welfare. Conversely, they don't do well when their parents are not committed to their welfare.**

Here's the problem I run into in case after case: both parents *say* they are committed to the welfare of their children, and both parents *say* they want what's best for their children, but then I see one or both of them saying things and doing things that are completely contrary to what is best for their kids. These may be things that put the children squarely in the middle, like "I know this is your night to be with your dad, but I'm inviting the neighbors over for a cookout. Wouldn't you like to stay here so you can swim and play with the other children?" Or things that might make the children feel bad or feel sorry for the parent, like the parent crying and saying, "I miss you so much when you aren't here." This puts the children in the role of being emotional caretakers for their parents, and it definitely is not good for children to have this burden.

So why do parents do this? Why do they say they want what's best for their kids and then act in ways that are harmful to them? Usually they just don't understand the effects of what they are saying or doing. Of course they want what's best for their children, but sometimes they just can't get out of their own way in order to do that. And sometimes they don't see how what they are doing could be harmful, so they just need some gentle education to gain that understanding.

My theory is that parents go in and out of an altered state of consciousness during this difficult time. This is the only explanation that makes sense to me of why normally thoughtful, considerate, and balanced people behave in ways practically unrecognizable to the people who know them. For some people it's like when you have the flu, and the doctor gives you some great drugs, and you lay on the sofa in la-la land for a couple of days, going in and out of awareness of the world around you. You are numb and don't really care what happens outside of your bit of consciousness, or you don't even know there is anything outside your bit of consciousness.

For others, it's like that roller coaster ride I mentioned. One minute you go along thinking you're coping pretty well with all the craziness going on in your life, and the next minute you have completely exploded all over your spouse or your children or some other innocent bystander without a clue as to what set you off. I remember a time during my separation when my husband came to my house. I do not remember now why he was there or even what we talked about. What I remember is being so angry when he left (but of course not showing it, haha!), and slamming the door so hard that the doorknob fell off, inside the house, at my feet, with a big thud, and we couldn't get out of the house. My 10 year-old daughter was just sitting there, looking at me, like I was from another planet. At that moment, I felt as if I were from another planet. I had entered that altered state of complete stupidness! How funny and ironic that we were "locked" inside our house as a result of my slamming the door. Could it be that I was also "locked" inside my own anger and frustration? Quite an insight from many years down the road.

I hope this story of what not to do is helpful and that knowing this could happen to you will keep you alert to it, and, therefore, help you to minimize the time you spend in that altered state. I recommend doing everything possible to avoid having your children look at you the way my daughter looked at me that day!

Divorce is such a complicated process, and there is so much emotion that needs to be sorted through, as you will see in Chapter Seven on the Four Divorces. Putting your children's needs ahead of your own isn't easy, and parents constantly have to check in with themselves to make sure they are doing this. Many parents also think "children are resilient" and they are not "that" affected by the divorce of their parents. My advice to all my clients who have children is to get them into counseling with an experienced counselor who can let the parents know how the children are doing and also help the parents see how their behavior is affecting the children. Obviously, as you may have picked up from my "what not to do" story, counseling for the parents isn't a bad idea either.

Doesn't it make sense that it's better for children to live in two peaceful homes rather than in one home that is in a constant state of warfare? Surely a good divorce is better for children than a bad marriage! At the risk of repeating myself, this is not to say that any of this is easy for the family, but if it is happening to your family, then at least be proactive, intentional, and grown up about it.

**Here are two critical factors to help you do what's best for your children:**

1. **Get along with the other parent as much as possible.** This means making a true effort to support the other parent in his or her relationship with the children and to be cooperative as needed for the sake of the children.

2. **When conflicts do arise, keep the children out of them.** They don't need to know the details of your situation. They don't need to know about other relationships, or money, or who did what to whom. What they need to know for sure is that both of you are there for them 100 percent, despite what's going on around them. Of course they will be sad about the divorce, but keeping them out of the fray will protect them psychologically and emotionally.

Dr. Constance Ahrons, a specialist in children and divorce and author of *We're Still Family*, says, "These two factors differentiate between the children who are and are not damaged by divorce." The good news in Dr. Ahrons' statement is that your children do not *have* to be damaged by your divorce. It is possible to divorce and still raise healthy, well-adjusted, and balanced children.

Here's how: do everything within your power to avoid high conflict between you and your spouse, angry outbursts in front of your children, and taking positions and engaging in power struggles with your spouse.

Instead, do everything in your power to remind yourself (as often as necessary) that your children need you and your spouse to work together to make decisions that are good for them. Be open to receiving information about what is best for your children so you and your spouse can make good decisions about them, rather than locking into a position about what you may think is best. And finally, remember that you, not your children, are getting the divorce, and while the divorce will change the form of your family, it doesn't need to, and shouldn't, change the way the children think and feel about each parent.

Again, it may be helpful to get a counselor involved to meet with you and your children to ensure they are adjusting to the changes as well and as normally as possible. Counselors can be the best resource for parents during this time. They can offer helpful information about what is and is not working for the children. Their only agenda is to help your kids adjust to the changes and move through this difficult time in an emotionally healthy manner. Children usually enjoy this new relationship. The counseling sessions are a safe place for them to talk about what's going on, how they're feeling, and to learn some valuable coping skills.

Here's a list of my **Top Ten Tips** to help you be the best parent possible during this time. Since many parents are just not aware of how their actions impact their children, these tips will open your eyes and raise your awareness to help you keep your focus on their needs:

1. **Remember that parents do not "visit" with their children. Children and parents live together, no matter how short or long a time they spend together. The language each one of you uses about the schedule can sometimes be problematic. Be sensitive to this.**

2. **Save negotiations and discussions with the other parent for a time when the children are not around and cannot overhear.**

3. **Learn how to communicate directly and respectfully with the other parent. Do not ask the children to carry messages to the other parent. They should not be in the middle of any of your disputes or be responsible for your communication.**

4. **Enjoy the time you have with your children. You can only do this well if you aren't obsessing about the time you don't have them with you!**

5. **Allow and encourage your children to have fun and enjoy being with the other parent. Remember that it's important for your child's normal emotional and**

psychological development to have a good relationship with both parents, regardless of where they live.

6. Say nice things about the other parent in front of the child. Making derogatory or disparaging remarks about the other parent is hurtful to the child and will often backfire on you. Allow your children to decide for themselves what kind of relationship they will have with each of you.

7. Assure your children that you and their other parent are taking care of them and will work out the details of their schedule. Never ask them where they want to live or whom they like better.

8. Always speak to the other parent in a civil, respectful way. If the conversation gets to the point where you are unable to do this, then end the conversation and take it up another time when things have calmed down.

9. Be flexible with schedule changes. Remember, your children benefit from seeing the two of you being cooperative, especially when it comes to taking care of their needs.

10. Always keep your promises to your children. This sends a powerful message to them that they can trust you and can have confidence that you are there for them.

For your convenience, benefit, and easy distribution to spouses and friends, I've made this list available for download at www.GracefulDivorceSolutions.com/book

I trust you've gotten my message loud and clear. If you truly want what is best for your children, you will diligently follow the two critical factors and tips set forth in this chapter. Clients always tell me they want what is best for their children, and I know they do, but often they don't act that way. The key is to be able to put your children's needs above your own, which is definitely challenging when all you might want to do is explode or crawl in a hole (or wring a certain person's neck!). But you can still put your children's needs first.

When you're having a hard time focusing on the children's needs, just step out of your own mind and into the mind of your child and answer the following questions. Insert your child or children's names, write out the sentences, and then write down whatever comes to your mind. By doing this exercise, you will experience an amazing shift in your thinking and a definite change in how you speak and act around your children.

(Again, if you are one who doesn't like to write in books, and since it's vitally important to this process that you take some time to think about and write out your responses to the following questions, I have provided a blank template of this for you at my website. Visit www.GracefulDivorceSolutions.com/book to download your copy. No excuses now for not doing these exercises!)

## ASK YOURSELF:

If I were _____ (my child), what would I want in this situation?

_____

_____

_____

_____

If I were _____ (my child), how would I want my Mom and Dad to be acting or reacting in this situation?

_____

_____

_____

_____

If I were _____ (my child), what could my parents do to ease my fear and sadness? (be specific)

_____

_____

_____

_____

If I were _____ (my child), what could my parents say to me that would be helpful?

_____

_____

_____

_____

When you are able to put yourself in your child's head and in your child's shoes, it will change the way you speak and act around your children. It is one of those selfless acts that parents are called upon to do as parents—to be the adult and allow your child to be a child.

Once you have done this, then ask yourself this question: **Who in my life can I seek out for support and kindness who can help us through this period in our lives?**

---

It's so much easier to manage this time with a good support system in place, whether it's family, friends, or professionals. Never hesitate to ask for help. None of us has all the answers, and all of us need help along the way from time to time.

# 6

# WHOSE FAULT IS IT ANYWAY? (THE MYTH OF WINNING!)

The question of fault comes up every time I meet with a new client, so I want to address this early on. Here are the comments I most often hear:

"He's the one having the affair! Why do I have to suffer?"

"She just up and left me. I can't let her get away with that."

"I didn't do anything wrong. Why should I have to leave my home?"

"He/she's been emotionally abusive to me for years. I want a divorce on the grounds of mental cruelty."

"I want to file on the grounds of adultery and take him/her to the cleaners!"

Whether you can get a fault based divorce varies from state to state. Many states no longer have divorces based on fault grounds. In other states, you can still get a divorce on a fault ground, which usually includes adultery, cruelty, desertion, or incarceration for more than a year. Theories on the value of having a fault vs. no-fault divorce abound, and it's not my intention to weigh in on this controversy. However, since I get questions from clients about this on a regular basis, it's important to address the issue.

I practice in an area where people can be divorced on a fault ground or they can get a no-fault divorce based on living separately for a specified period of time, depending on whether or not they have minor children. In my area, if you can prove adultery, then you can get a final divorce immediately, or whenever you can get before a judge to make your case, which is seldom anything but immediate. The court dockets are jammed full and nothing happens quickly when you are trying to set cases for trial.

The real question for you is whether fault makes a difference in your case. Does it matter to a judge whether your spouse committed adultery, or left you, or was cruel to you? This is what I call the "myth of winning." First of all, it's not easy to prove any of these grounds. If you are able to prove your spouse's fault in court and the judge does find your spouse at fault, what does that get you? Will he or she be punished, and will you get a better deal in the end? Do you really "win" anything? The answer depends on your judge and your jurisdiction.

In most jurisdictions, the trend is toward less and less emphasis on fault. Even when a judge finds fault, it's usually just one of ten or more factors (as you will see in the lists in Chapter Eleven) that are considered when dividing the marital property, awarding spousal support, or determining custody. That should give you an idea of how much emphasis a judge gives to the bad behavior of your spouse—about ten percent overall. Not great odds.

Of course, there are extreme cases, where one spouse may be having an affair, or a number of affairs, and/or using marital monies inappropriately, and the evidence is obvious, overwhelming, and flagrant, but those are not the norm. The norm is that a marriage has broken down, one spouse or the other has an affair or moves out and then pursues a divorce. The norm is that if fault becomes an issue, the case becomes one of "he said/she said," meaning both parties are hurling allegations of fault against the other, to the point where the case becomes so mucked up the judge has no idea whom to believe. What do judges do when there isn't enough evidence to support either side's story and they can't figure out whom to believe? They punt. They dismiss all fault grounds alleged by both sides and proceed to decide the rest of the case. You are back to square one. You have gained nothing, you've likely expended tremendous financial and emotional resources, and have done tremendous damage in the process.

I tell my clients that unless they have some documented evidence that could prove a fault ground, it's a waste of time and money to go down that road. The truth is there is almost nothing to be gained by claiming fault and a great deal to lose in terms of time, money, and stress. Instead, I encourage my clients to get back to the Big Picture of what they want their lives to look like when the divorce is over and to keep their focus on that picture. The truth is that if there is a provable fault ground, there was already a breakdown in the marriage. If the marriage was stable, honest, and committed, the breakdown would not have occurred. This is generally true unless there are issues of addiction, abuse, or mental illness. Once they take time to reflect on this, most clients acknowledge that this is true for them and see the reality of the "myth of winning."

This may sound direct and blunt, and it is, but it's also the truth. If a marriage is over, it's over. You cannot make someone stay in a relationship against his or her will. Furthermore, if a marriage isn't working, it's seldom just one person's fault. **Learning to be accountable for your role in what happened in the marriage goes a long way toward ending the marriage in a more civilized way, and also toward helping you to recover and to move forward in a healthy and balanced manner.** Working with the right professionals can help you do this. And that is what this book is about—learning how to end your marriage in a civilized way so you and your family not only survive the process, but thrive.

(Again, if you are one who doesn't like to write in books, and since it's vitally important to this process that you take some time to think about and write out your responses to the following questions, I have provided a blank template of this for you at my website. Visit www.GracefulDivorceSolutions.com/book to download your copy. No excuses now for not doing these exercises!)

### *ASK YOURSELF:*

What happened in my marriage?

_____

_____

_____

_____

_____

_____

What role did I play to get where I am now?

_____

_____

_____

_____

_____

_____

What role did my spouse play?

_____

_____

_____

_____

_____

What do I want now? Do I want to try to make my marriage work?

_____

_____

_____

_____

_____

Is my spouse willing to try to make the marriage work?

_____

_____

_____

_____

_____

If so, am I/we willing to get the help I/we need?

_____

_____

_____

_____

If not, am I/we willing to discuss with my spouse where to go from here?

_____

_____

_____

_____

# 7

## THE FOUR DIVORCES:

### HOW TO PREPARE YOURSELF TO DO DIVORCE BETTER

Most people going through a divorce have certain expectations. They expect to go from being married to being unmarried. But how do they get there? Just like going on a trip, they have to figure out how to get from Point A to Point B. Unfortunately, often a trip that seems well-planned can somehow go off track and take on a life of its own.

Why is it so hard? When and how did it get so complicated? Why do some people become unrecognizable to their spouses and friends?

Here's the answer. We think of divorce as **a single event.** A person gets divorced and it's done, as if it were a one-time happening. The truth is there are really Four Divorces happening

*process*

all at the *same* time, *and* over a *period* of time. Where previous chapters have discussed how the legal system is broken, this chapter explains what most people don't get about divorce— that there is so much more involved than just the legal piece.

### The Four Divorces are:

- **The Legal Divorce**

- **The Financial Divorce**

- **The Social Divorce**

- **The Emotional Divorce**

Everyone who gets divorced goes through each of these divorces. Since we are all individuals, we go through them in different ways and over different periods of time. Some are faster, some are slower. They are easier for some, and harder for others. As you and your spouse experience each of these divorces at your own pace, problems may come up which make communication difficult and disrupt attempts at settlement.

**Once you see how the Four Divorces interact, and how critical it is to go through each one, you will be better prepared to deal with your own divorce process.**

Let's take a look at each of these divorces and examine how they affect your overall experience of divorce.

## THE LEGAL DIVORCE

The Legal Divorce is what most people think of when they think of "divorce." It is simply the legal framework for finalizing your divorce. Papers are filed in the court initiating the process, certain procedures have to be followed, and then a judge will sign a document stating that you are officially divorced. The process varies by state.

A divorce is either contested or uncontested. A contested divorce is when the parties haven't been able to reach an agreement on the issues involved (see Chapter Twelve for specifics). The case ends up in litigation with a judge making all the decisions. One common misconception I hear is, "My husband says he'll never give me a divorce. What can I do?" In most states you can be divorced after you've been separated a certain period of time whether or not your spouse agrees to the divorce. The key is the time period of actual separation. However, if you have been separated the required time period, but you are still not able to agree on the issues in your case, like division of property or custody, then your case is contested and has to go to court to be finalized.

*? separation agreement*

An uncontested divorce is when both of you agree on how to resolve the issues regarding children, support, and division of property, and you have a written agreement which both of you have signed. When you are able to do this, then the legal divorce doesn't take as long to complete. It's also less expensive and less stressful than the contested divorce, and it can be finalized without going to court at all in most states.

## THE FINANCIAL DIVORCE

The Financial Divorce obviously deals with your money, what you own, and what you owe. You need to make decisions about how to divide your marital assets and liabilities. These decisions can be difficult, as now the income that used to support one household will be supporting two. This is a harsh reality for many divorcing couples.

Being open, honest, and cooperative about the marital assets and liabilities makes this part of the divorce go more smoothly. If you have trouble getting through one of the Four Divorces, it's unlikely you'll be able to make the financial decisions necessary to complete the divorce process. For example, if friends or family members (the Social Divorce) are telling you to "take him/her to the cleaners," and you allow *their* agenda to control the process, you won't be able to resolve the Financial Divorce in either mediation or collaboration.

What happens if you can't resolve and have to take your divorce to court? You end up spending money on legal fees that should otherwise be going into your pocket and your spouse's pocket. On the other hand, if you work together in either mediation or collaboration, you can create your own custom solutions that set yourselves and your children up financially for the best divorce situation possible. I'm an advocate for *you* keeping as much of *your* money as possible!

## THE SOCIAL DIVORCE

The Social Divorce deals with how your friends and family adjust to the fact that you and your spouse are no longer together. Divorce is a family affair. Everyone around you is affected. Your friends, family, and co-workers have related to you and your spouse as a couple, and now they must learn to relate to each of you as single individuals. Each person reacts differently and on his or her own time-table. Be respectful and allow people to go through their own adjustments to the end of your relationship.

It's helpful to keep your family and friends out of your divorce and keep the focus on what is best for you and your children. Your family and friends likely have strong feelings and support you, but their well-meaning advice often makes things worse.

I recommend using mediation or collaboration to help keep other people's agendas from controlling what happens in your divorce. When using either of these processes, you have the final say regarding your agreements. You learn effective ways of communicating with your spouse. Family members can be included in these conversations if necessary, but remember, this is your divorce. Don't let your friends' and family's agendas derail your process.

## THE EMOTIONAL DIVORCE

This is the most difficult of the Four Divorces and the one that catches people off guard. Ending a marriage feels a lot like losing a loved one—it's a loss you must grieve. If you've ever lost someone close to you, you know what this is like.

The stages of grieving are:

- **Denial and Shock**—"This can't be happening to me. We can figure this out."

- **Anger**— "I can't believe you're doing this to me! It's not fair."

- **Bargaining**—"I'll change and make this stop."

- **Sadness and Depression**—"This is really happening. What will I do? How will I live?"

- **Acceptance**—"This is the way it is. I'll be just fine. It's time for me to get on with my life."

Everyone goes through the emotional phase of divorce differently, just like everyone grieves in his or her own unique way. And, quite honestly, although you go through the grieving process like you do when a loved one dies, this is not quite the same because *this* person has not died. He or she is still on the planet, maybe living just down the street, or across town with a new love. So not only do you grieve the loss of your spouse, partner, lifestyle, and dreams, but now you also have to figure out how to keep walking around on the planet with this other person in a socially acceptable way.

The problem is it's difficult to think clearly and to make good decisions when you're in the early stages of this grief and recovery process. **Being aware that it *is* a process, and knowing *where you are* in the process, is critical to you being able to make the best choices for you.** Also, understanding that your spouse is going through this as well can better help you understand his or her behavior. This is especially important during settlement negotiations.

It makes a difference, too, whether you are the one initiating the divorce (the "Leaver") or the one being left (the "Leavee"). If you are the Leaver, you've been thinking about this for some time and are ahead of your spouse emotionally. A psychologist once told me that the person who is leaving the relationship is usually about two years ahead in this process. You've been through the stages above and have reached the acceptance stage. You're ready for the divorce to be over and to move on with your life. You're ready to sit down and work out an agreement.

If you are the Leavee, you may be shocked and surprised by your spouse's decision to separate. You do everything you can to keep your spouse from leaving, and you resist any actions that could lead to a divorce. You're in the early stages of the grieving process and need time to catch up to your spouse.

You're definitely not ready to sit down to negotiate, and you will tend to delay or sabotage the process whenever possible. Or you may have the opposite response, where you are in such shock that you agree to any terms proposed in order not to have to deal with the situation, and later, you have tremendous regret for your impulsive decisions. Unfortunately, usually a signed agreement is a done deal unless you can show that your spouse held a gun to your head to get you to sign it.

In order to understand better the Leaver and the Leavee, imagine first that you are the Leaver. Mentally and emotionally, you are gone. You have left the marriage in every way except physically. You're still there. But how many times have you walked through the rooms in your house and thought about which items you would like to take and which you would leave? How many times have you scribbled out a budget and wondered whether you would be able to make it on your own? How many times have you dreamed of other places you would like to live? How many times have you had the conversation in your head with your spouse about maybe this isn't working and maybe we should separate, wishing and hoping he or she would just agree it wasn't working anymore, but knowing that the proverbial poop is going to hit the fan, and dreading that moment? How long do you stay in this place before stepping up and speaking what is true for you and probably what is best for both of you?

And now imagine that you are the Leavee. A bomb has just dropped on your world. You never even saw it coming. You thought, "Sure, we have some problems, but we're okay. It'll get better. This too shall pass." But it didn't pass and the unthinkable has happened. Your spouse has told you he or she wants to separate or divorce, and you feel like someone has just ripped out your insides. What will you do now? How will you get through this? What will people think? How dare he or she? And these thoughts go on and on and around and around until you feel like you're losing your mind. The emotions of hurt, fear, humiliation, anger, and rage are all wrapped up nice and tight within you, ready to leak out in little bits or explode in huge chunks at unacceptable and inappropriate times, and it all feels like it's completely out of your control. Enter that altered state feeling once again.

Do you see how helpful it can be to recognize where you are in the process, and then to recognize where your spouse is in the process? And also, if you can muster it up at this difficult time, to have some empathy and compassion for the other? I admit, that may be too much to ask, but just thinking about it can be helpful.

If you're the Leaver, recognize that your spouse needs time to process what is going on. Give your spouse space and time to catch up with you. If you're the Leavee, find a good counselor who can support you and help you understand how you got to where you are. Recognize that you need time to process this dramatic life change. Take steps to allow yourself time and space to process everything.

How you negotiate and communicate with one another during your divorce is *always* impacted by where each of you is in the Emotional Divorce. If the two of you are in very different places, you need to allow some time to pass before trying to negotiate anything except the most pressing matters.

In most cases, I recommend mediation or collaboration as the best choices for resolution because it allows you to take time-outs as needed and then to resume the process when the time is right. By understanding where you and your spouse are in each of the Four Divorces, you will be able to make conscious choices as you go along. You will be more mindful and thoughtful, better able to maintain your emotional balance, and able to make informed and responsible decisions.

Take some time to reflect on the following questions. Then take out your journal and write out your answers in as much detail as possible.

(Again, if you are one who doesn't like to write in books, and since it's vitally important to this process that you take some time to think about and write out your responses to the following questions, I have provided a blank template of this for you at my website. Visit www.GracefulDivorceSolutions.com/book

to download your copy. No excuses now for not doing these exercises!)

### *ASK YOURSELF:*

Where do I fall in the Emotional Divorce? Am I the Leaver or the Leavee?

_____

_____

_____

_____

If I'm the one who left, do I need to slow things down and give my spouse a chance to catch up? What's going on now that would help me answer this question?

_____

_____

_____

_____

If I'm the one who was left, what do I need to do to get the help and support I need so I can cope with what's going on in the best way possible?

_____

_____

_____

_____

Am I willing to seek out the help I need? If not, why not?

_____

_____

_____

_____

_____

How am I handling other family members and the Social Divorce?

_____

_____

_____

_____

_____

Am I making efforts to maintain relationships?

_____

_____

_____

_____

How do the Four Divorces affect the different areas of my situation?

_____

_____

_____

_____

_____

What can I take from this chapter that will help me in my own divorce situation?

_____

_____

_____

_____

# 8

# THE OPTIONS—
# A BLUEPRINT FOR CHANGE

If and when you decide that divorce is inevitable for you, what then? People come to this place in many different ways. Some of my clients walk in my door ready to pursue a divorce. Others come in just wanting information but not ready to take action. Many hope to work things out with their spouses, but they want to know what their options are if things don't work out.

This is smart. It's good to know what to expect, it's good to know what to think about, and it's good to be prepared. When I meet with clients who are unsure about the future of their relationships, the first thing I suggest is counseling, individually and with their spouses, if possible. If they are open to this, couples counseling can help them to work through their issues or to realize that they aren't able to work through their issues.

Individually, counseling can help clients better understand their relationships and decide what they want to have happen, as well as to settle on the best course of action for them.

Sometimes I find clients are waiting to see what their spouses want before deciding what they want themselves. I'm sure this is because the whole idea of divorcing and all the change it means is so big for some people, they just can't even think about going there unless they feel like they have no choice. And if their spouses make that decision, then they don't have to make the choice. It's made for them!

I encourage my clients to figure out what *they* want first, and not wait for their spouses to make their decisions. If they are already sitting in my office, there are probably some pretty significant issues that aren't being resolved. Often the clients sitting in my office who are waiting for their spouses to make the call are really not happy or fulfilled in their relationships, but just very fearful about their futures if they follow their hearts and do what they feel is truly best for them. Sometimes my job is simply to help them see their situations differently, mostly by helping them see that they do have choices. Despite what they may think at the time, they are not powerless regarding their current situations, and there is life after divorce.

Once we talk about their situations, then we will talk about their options. If they decide to pursue divorce, what's the next step? Most people think the next step is to meet with a lawyer, pay a retainer, and walk out of the lawyer's office with a big

"Whew! Sure glad I don't have to worry about *that* anymore!" It might sound ridiculous to you, but many people do this. They turn all their power over to the lawyer without knowing why they are doing this and what the consequences will be.

Why is it this way? I think it's because people are afraid, they're emotional, they don't know what to expect, and they don't know what to do.

After all, the legal system can be intimidating. Lawyers and judges can be intimidating. Clients feel vulnerable, and unfortunately, many lawyers capitalize on that vulnerability. I'm not saying all lawyers intend this or do so. What I'm saying is this is the way the system has evolved, and it isn't working. Perhaps it's time to consider other, more expansive and effective options.

You might still pay the big retainer and hire the big gun lawyer. That's okay too. Some cases require that, like those discussed in Chapter Eleven. There is no "one size fits all" choice here. However, if you go through the steps as I have outlined in this book, you will see that you can do your divorce better by being more involved in your process.

Think about how similar this thinking is to how we are becoming more and more involved and proactive in our own health care. If you have health problems, do you believe and do everything your doctor says, or do you do your own investigation as well? Who knows *you* better than *you*? Just because a doctor recommends a course of treatment, does that mean it's the best choice for you? Maybe, but maybe not. Doctors should give you information, lay out your options, and give you the benefit of their experience, but you have to make the ultimate decision about how to proceed.

It's the same thing with your lawyer. If you are having legal problems, do not believe and do everything your lawyer says. Do your own investigation and take a proactive role in your own case. Just as in your health care, only *you* know what is best for *you*. You should depend on lawyers to give you information, to lay out your options, and to give you the benefit of their experiences, but you must decide which direction to go from there. Your agenda, not the lawyer's, is the only one that matters.

I will now get off my soapbox and explain your options. They cover a broad, continuous spectrum, from the most intrusive and expensive, involving more professional intervention and less privacy and control, to those that are the least intrusive and allow the most privacy and control. Because every separating/divorcing couple is different, every case is different. The professionals you choose to help you, and how you use their help, will significantly affect how your divorce proceeds.

When I'm talking with people and explaining their different process options, I say to them, "You might not agree on what your relationship should be like, or how to discipline your children or where they should live, or how to handle your money, but you *can* agree on what process to use to resolve those issues and to divorce."

**Here are the options on the divorce continuum:**

**1. Litigation**

**2. Lawyer/Lawyer Negotiation**

**3. Mediation**

**4. Collaboration**

**5. Do It Yourself**

Let's take a look at each option now in depth.

## OPTION ONE—LITIGATION = war

### Litigation at a Glance

- Expensive

- Focus is on "winning" and "getting the best deal"

- Needs of children are often overlooked

- Court docket dictates the pacing of your case

- Public has access/no privacy

### The Details

Litigation is when you go to court and a judge decides your case for you. One or both parties go out and hire the best litigators they can find to make sure they get the best deal in the divorce. The parties see their divorce as either winning or losing. They are typically driven by strong emotions of fear, anger, or guilt. As a result, they tend to take extreme positions and look to the court system for justice and revenge. In short, it's war.

This is the most expensive form of dispute resolution, both emotionally and financially. It's destructive for both parties. These cases can and do go on for years, with little satisfaction achieved by either side. The adversarial process rarely settles the issues between the parties. And, let's face it—it's a lousy way to prepare for life after divorce.

If you have children, going to court is destructive for them also. You won't learn the skills you need to be able to communicate with your child's other parent, or to move past your conflict in order to concentrate on your children.

Although I seldom recommend litigation, there are times when it's necessary and unavoidable. These include the following:

1. When there is a **history of domestic violence** in the relationship and there is an issue of safety for either you or your spouse or your children.

2. When there is a **history of mental illness or personality disorder** which makes it impossible to negotiate or communicate effectively.

3. When one spouse takes action by **filing court documents** alleging a fault ground for divorce and setting trial dates,

the other spouse has no alternative but to engage in the legal battle, unless the couple can reach an agreement to stop the court action and begin another dispute resolution process like mediation or collaboration.

For more information on the effects of litigating your divorce, see Chapter Ten and for more information on dealing with domestic violence, mental illness, and addiction issues, see Chapter Eleven.

### *Case in Point—David and Jane*

*David and Jane had three children, ages 14, 11, and 7. Jane came to me after getting a protective order against David. There had been problems in the marriage for a number of years. David was abusive and controlling. Jane felt powerless and didn't know what to do about it. As often happens, she finally reached a breaking point because of something David had done which, this time, involved the children. She got some much-needed support and took action.*

*Because there was a history of domestic violence, and because David also had some mental health issues, this was a case that ended up in litigation. What we knew was that David had suffered a head injury at some point in his past that had impacted his ability to reason and his thinking in ways not quite understood, except that it had gotten progressively worse over the years. His behavior had become more and more unpredictable and volatile. His words and actions were extremely self-centered and self-involved, and he had a complete lack of empathy for anyone else. In particular, he had no concept of how the things he was saying and the way he was behaving were impacting his children. It was clear that it was all about him, and only him. He would say how much he loved and missed his children, and I believe that in his own head he truly did, but there was a huge disconnect there between this sentiment and his actions.*

*We tried to negotiate a settlement agreement with David, but because of his mental health issues, it was impossible. One minute he was telling Jane that he loved her and was begging her to come back to him, and the next he was telling the children their mother was a whore and a slut, and that they were going to live with him and never see her again because he was going to "take her out." The children were traumatized by his erratic behavior and fearful that their father was going to harm their mother. Naturally the more he persisted with this, the more protective they became of their mother and the angrier they were at him.*

*David's lawyer tried to get David to see how his behavior was affecting the children and to see the value in our settlement proposals, but to no avail. Even though Jane had only worked part-time off and on throughout the marriage, and David ran a lucrative business, he could not see why he had to pay her any support or give her any of the marital assets. He was stubborn, resistant, and unreasonable throughout the case, and left us no choice but to go to court.*

*The results were devastating for this family. The legal fees for both were exorbitant. It was two years before the case was finally over, and this extremely long time before resolution was especially difficult for the children. They had a Guardian ad litem appointed for them (a lawyer appointed by the court to represent the best interests of the children), but it didn't seem to matter how many times she assured them they would not be taken from their mother, they still had a fear that their father might get their custody in court. After all, he told them this on a regular basis. That fear caused tremendous stress and anxiety for the children and impacted their behavior as well as their schoolwork. Ultimately, when the case was over, they were hugely relieved that their mother had their custody, but they had little interest in continuing any relationship with their father. This was very unfortunate for the children and would have lasting emotional and psychological effects on them.*

## OPTION TWO—LAWYER/LAWYER NEGOTIATION

### Lawyer/Lawyer Negotiation At A Glance

- Lawyer speaks for the client—becomes the "mouthpiece"

- Litigation is always looming if settlement is not reached

- Can be expensive and time consuming

- Stressful to the family

- Legal issues may get resolved, but emotional issues remain

### The Details

Lawyer/Lawyer Negotiation is actually what happens in most cases where the clients go out and hire lawyers to represent them in their divorce. For whatever reasons, they were unable to work it out themselves and haven't elected to try mediation or collaboration. Often they just aren't aware there is any other way to go or that they have options.

In these situations, each client hires a lawyer to help him or her negotiate a settlement, and then the lawyers talk to each other. The clients no longer need to talk to one another because the lawyers are their "mouthpieces." The retained lawyers may be good at settlement negotiation or they may be good at litigation, so how the case goes depends on what the lawyers like to do or are best at. The clients may *think* they are working on settlement. Sometimes the communication between lawyer and client is not clear.

The problem with this option is that the door to litigation is always open if they are not able to settle. This "open door to litigation" is a hook that hangs out there, and in my experience, it often prevents the case from settling because the lawyers continue the "posturing" game. When one side or the other doesn't negotiate reasonably, these cases end up escalating. Lawyer/Lawyer negotiation, then, is often just a precursor to litigation.

In the lawyer-lawyer negotiation, sometimes lawyers will negotiate by sending letters or property settlement proposals back and forth, and sometimes they try to get the clients to meet together in four-way meetings. Because the case might not settle and litigation may be necessary, at the same time as the lawyers are trying to negotiate settlement, they are also preparing for court and positioning their clients to be in the best possible situation. It's like sitting down for a peace treaty while each country continues to stockpile ammunition!

Sometimes it works, but more often it doesn't. In the end, the lawyers and couple may reach an agreement and get the legal issues resolved, but the emotional and psychological issues are seldom resolved. Clients have not learned how to communicate effectively, relationships are not maintained, and children are not protected.

### *Case in Point—Mike and Angela*

*Mike and Angela had only been married a few years when Angela came to see me. She was devastated after discovering some disturbing and incriminating emails and pictures on the Internet when Mike was off on a business trip.*

*Because they had been married such a short time and didn't have children, there wasn't much that needed to be resolved in terms of the legal divorce. Both of them had professional jobs and good incomes, so spousal support was not an issue. Angela had moved into Mike's home before they got married, and they had each put some of their own money into the house. When they got married, they refinanced the home, used some of that money for improvements, and titled the house in both names. Figuring out how to divide the equity in the house was the issue.*

*Also, an issue for Angela was what to do with the information she had discovered. She felt hurt and betrayed and a part of her wanted to file a divorce on fault grounds. The other part of her had hopes that maybe they could work it out. Mike promised her he would go to counseling and work on their marriage, and when she discovered one day that he really hadn't made any changes at all, she reached her limit and told me she was "done." She wanted to file the divorce so Mike would know, and hopefully admit to her, that he had been wrong and that he had betrayed her in the marriage. She also wanted him to know that she had strong evidence to prove her case. She wasn't prepared, though, for the counterclaim filed against her in response. It made her out to be a screaming, crazy, emotionally damaged person. She was shocked and upset, and the case escalated quickly.*

*Even though Angela was upset and wanted the world to know what Mike had done, she was also anxious to get on with her life, which meant she had to get her case resolved and the divorce finalized. Unfortunately, a court date could not be set regarding the division of equity in the house until they had been separated for a year, so we either had to wait until the year was up or try to negotiate a settlement.*

*We began some lawyer-lawyer negotiations to try to get the case settled. We prepared a settlement proposal that Angela felt was a fair and equal division of the equity in the home, even though she felt like she deserved more based on what he had done. The response received was not even close to what she had offered, and, in fact, didn't offer Angela any of the equity in the home. Angela viewed the response as completely unreasonable and unacceptable, and the case stagnated again. As much as she wanted the divorce to be over, she was not willing to walk away from what she felt she was legally entitled to. Six months later the case was settled, the day before court, for an amount very close (within $1,000) to what she had offered more than six months prior. It probably cost Mike and Angela about $5,000 each in additional legal fees to reach the same settlement offered initially.*

*As is typical in the lawyer-lawyer negotiation cases when the lawyers are ultimately preparing for court, both Mike and Angela ended up with significantly higher attorney fees than necessary, the case dragged on much longer than it should have, and the stress had a detrimental impact on everyone involved.*

## OPTION THREE—COLLABORATIVE DIVORCE

### Collaborative Divorce at a Glance

- Agreement not to go to court

- Promotes mutual respect

- Emphasizes the needs of the children

- Clients control the process and make final decisions

- Process and discussions are kept private

- Communication is open and constructive

- Focuses on needs and interests of clients and the family

- Utilizes a problem solving approach

## The Details

Collaborative Divorce is the newest form of divorce dispute resolution. Despite the efforts of enthusiastic lawyers who now practice collaborative divorce, many people have still not heard of this process. It's different from mediation in that each client has his or her own lawyer in the room as personal *advisor* and *advocate*. In mediation, the Mediator's job is to help you reach an agreement, but he or she may *not* give legal advice or advocate for either side. The collaborative lawyer may do both.

The crux of the collaborative process is that the clients sign a contract that they **will not go to court** and that they will participate openly and honestly. It's referred to as a **transparent process**. There are no "taking of positions" or trying to "hide the ball" as in the traditional litigated case. From the beginning, settlement is the **only** agenda. If settlement is not reached and the process breaks down, the collaborative lawyers must withdraw from representing the clients and the clients have to hire new attorneys. This is perhaps the only downside to this process. Ending the process and hiring new lawyers takes time and money. However, it also provides the biggest incentive to both the lawyers *and* the clients to stay with the process and reach an acceptable settlement both sides feel they can live with.

In a Collaborative Divorce, each client has his or her own lawyer who is trained in a skill set that combines resolving disputes with client advocacy and advising. This process was partially developed in the late 1980s by a Minnesota lawyer named Stu Webb who was so disillusioned with the conventional divorce process that he seriously considered leaving the law. As a last resort, he decided to encourage his clients to try what he thought was a better way of divorcing, a way which allowed the clients to maintain their integrity, dignity, and to preserve their important relationships. They had to agree at the outset not to go to court and to resolve their issues according to the process he developed. At the same time, two professionals in California, Pauline Tesler and Peggy Thompson, an attorney and a mental health professional, were developing the same concept in their approach to cases. This process is now known as Collaborative Divorce and has spread worldwide. Check out the Recommended Reading and Resources section at the end of this book for information on the excellent books on collaborative divorce written by these individuals.

The goal of Collaborative Divorce is to develop respectful relationships, solve problems together, and avoid going to court.

The process is transparent, meaning there is full and complete disclosure by the clients, and the attorneys give their advice and experience in the presence of everyone during the meetings. For example, during a collaborative meeting, if I think my client is being unreasonable in her demands or has unreasonable expectations, I will tell her that. I will explain the law and my experience with the particular issue, and I will ask the other lawyer to comment regarding his or her experience. Both clients benefit from hearing the advice and experience of both lawyers. A trusting relationship develops and the group works together as a team for the benefit of the family members in supporting them through the divorce process.

The newest evolution in collaborative divorce is a comprehensive approach referred to as the Collaborative Divorce Team. Where collaborative divorce initially involved only the two clients and two trained collaborative lawyers, a full collaborative team can now include the two lawyers, one or two Divorce Coaches, a Child Specialist, and a Financial Specialist.

This process is effective because it helps clients come up with their own settlement agreements specific to their needs and concerns while being supported by a team of professionals. The team of professionals gives them advice, answers their questions, and helps to keep them on track to achieve their goals as individuals and as a family. At the beginning of the process, the professionals help the couple to craft a mission statement for them and for their children. The team will help keep the couple focused on this throughout the process.

Collaborative divorce works for people who want a peaceful resolution to their differences and who want to maintain a cooperative and mutually respectful relationship, but who need the support of trained professionals to accomplish this. The process is not for everyone, but it's for almost everyone.

How do you know if collaboration is the best choice for you? Read on. Chapter Nine gives you more details about the process and should answer any other questions you have. The bottom line is that Collaborative Divorce is the way to go for most people. Most often it takes less time, costs less money, and causes less stress than any of your other process choices, while also providing the emotional, financial, and legal support that is so important for your family during this time.

### _Case In Point—Jim and Carolyn_

_Jim and Carolyn had two children and had been married about 10 years. They were devoted to their children and came to the collaborative process primarily to make sure they protected them as much as possible. Neither of them really understood what had happened in their marriage. They just knew they weren't happy together and it was beginning to affect the whole family._

_Once Jim and Carolyn had each hired a collaborative lawyer, their next step was to decide whom else they needed on their_ *collaborative team in order to help get them where they said they wanted to go. They had similar goals for their divorce. They both wanted to:*

- *Protect their children as much as possible and come up with a parenting plan that would meet the needs of the children and also maximize each parent's time with them.*

- *Keep the children in the marital home, at least for now, until other decisions could be made about division of assets.*

- *Figure out how to divide up their assets in a way that would enable each of them to be able to have a suitable place for the children when they were with them.*

- *Maintain financial security for the future.*

*Because their number one priority was protecting their children, and because they had so many questions about what was best for them, they both agreed to include a Child Specialist on the team. The Child Specialist met with them and with the children before the first full team meeting. She was able to help answer questions for Jim and Carolyn about what was best for the children and what they needed, and she was able to be the voice of the children in the meetings. She helped Jim and Carolyn come up with a parenting plan which worked well for everyone involved and significantly reduced the stress everyone was feeling, especially the children, about what was going to happen with them. Once this piece was resolved in such a positive way, Jim and Carolyn were able to focus on other issues that needed to be resolved.*

*Because the last few years of the marriage had been somewhat strained and Jim and Carolyn were not good at talking with each other, they also agreed that it would be beneficial to hire a Divorce Coach. The Divorce Coach is the Communication Specialist in the process. He met with each of them prior to the first meeting and was extremely effective in teaching them some communication techniques that made an immediate difference in how they interacted and communicated. The Divorce Coach attended all the meetings and helped them to keep their conversations moving forward effectively. For Carolyn, she had to learn how to voice what she really wanted in ways Jim could hear. And for Jim, he had to learn how to listen effectively and not just assume he knew what she was thinking. It was helpful to both of them, especially in terms of setting them up for better communication after their divorce.*

*Finally, because they had some complicated financial issues and budgeting concerns, they decided to hire a Financial Specialist. The Financial Specialist helped them gather all the information they needed in order to get an accurate picture of their assets and their liabilities. He was able to bring this to a full team meeting for discussion and significantly reduced the time that would have been involved in figuring out this piece.*

*Although not all collaborative cases go this smoothly, this one was amazing, mostly because Jim and Carolyn were determined to keep the peace as much as possible, to be fair with each other regarding their money and assets, and to do their divorce in a way that would have as little impact on their children as possible. Because they agreed to bring onto the team the Child Specialist, the Divorce Coach, and the Financial Specialist, they had a professional team in place who were experts in their areas and who could help them achieve their goals quite efficiently.*

*Jim and Carolyn were able to complete the process and reach an agreement in five full team meetings. Even with all the professionals involved, the whole process was less expensive, took less time, and was less stressful than if they had gone through litigation. At the last meeting when the agreement was signed, Jim and Carolyn both expressed how pleased they were with how the process had worked for them and how happy they were because the children were doing so well and had adjusted fairly easily to all the changes in their lives.*

## OPTION FOUR—MEDIATION

### Mediation at a Glance

- Can resolve divorce issues without lawyers or court

- Saves time and money

- Less stressful

- Private

- Clients maintain control

### The Details

Moving along the divorce continuum, mediation is a process that can allow a great amount of privacy and control.

You and your spouse can use the mediation process with or without lawyers. A mediator is a neutral third party trained to facilitate conversations and agreements. The mediator has no decision-making authority power in the process, and may not give legal advice, but helps the parties voluntarily to reach a mutually acceptable resolution of their issues. The mediator may be a lawyer or someone else trained in the process. The mediator structures the mediation to help you and your spouse successfully negotiate an agreement.

Mediation usually follows a five-stage sequence. Most divorce mediations take from three to five sessions, depending on the complexity of the issues to be resolved.

The five stages typically followed are:

1. **Introduction**—You give the mediator background on your situation and the mediator explains the process to you.

2. **Information gathering**—You may prepare worksheets provided by the mediator regarding monthly income and expenses. You may be asked to bring in financial documents regarding assets, debts, and income for a true picture of the marital estate. Remember, you need to have complete information in order to negotiate a successful settlement.

3. **Framing**—The Mediator asks you and your spouse what you each think the settlement should be, and to explain

your reasons for your proposal. This is where you each discuss your interests, needs, and goals as they relate to the division of property, custody, and support. The Mediator's goal is to help you both find a resolution that meets each of your most important interests, needs, and goals.

4. **Negotiating**—Once you and your spouse both know and understand your own and your spouse's priorities in terms of interest, needs, and goals, you are ready to consider options. In this stage you explore different ways of settlement. You and your spouse discuss and evaluate options with the goal of narrowing your options to those that best meet each of your interests, needs, and goals. Getting to this point requires each of you to make compromises. The best agreement is often defined as one in which neither party gets everything he or she wants, but the final product is "acceptable" to both.

5. **Concluding**—Once settlement is reached, the tentative agreement is put into writing and circulated for review. The mediator likely encourages each of you to take the agreement to a lawyer for review.

In general, mediation takes less time and is less expensive than litigation. It works well when there is a balance of power in the relationship and when the issues are not overly complicated. It also works well when the parties need some help in getting to an acceptable agreement, but they still want to maintain control of the pacing of their case and may not want to involve lawyers and the courts.

Mediation would not be the best process choice in a situation where there is an imbalance of power in the relationship, or where there is a history of physical or emotional abuse. If this is the case, one of the parties is likely to be intimidated by the other party and, therefore, likely to do whatever the other says in order to avoid conflict and keep the peace. The mediator may not even recognize this is going on. The result is an unfair agreement. Collaboration would be a better process choice for a person in this scenario because each individual would have his or her own lawyer in the room at all times and have the benefit of the lawyer's advice and advocacy. The lawyer would also be a buffer and provide support for the client, enabling the client to speak up in a safe environment.

Once an agreement is reached and signed, it will then be filed with the court as part of the divorce. If you are interested in this process, be sure to do your homework and find a mediator with excellent training, skills, and experience so the process will be effective and successful for you. Finding the right mediator is a lot like choosing the right lawyer for you. The most important consideration is experience. Mediation is an art. The more experience a person has, the better he or she is likely to be. You want someone who is skilled at listening, communicating, and asking powerful and insightful questions. You also want someone who is knowledgeable about divorce.

Most mediators for divorce are either therapists or lawyers. If you use a lawyer-mediator, then you will have someone whom you know understands the divorce process and any legal complications of your case, as well as someone who can draft a legally binding divorce agreement once you reach a resolution. Also, a good mediator will recommend that lawyers for both sides review the agreement before it's signed. They often will refer you to mediation-friendly lawyers who will review your agreement for any legal oversights without undermining your decision to resolve your case through mediation.

The best way to find a mediator is to ask for referrals from people you know who have been through mediation. Mental health agencies and family therapists are also a good source for referrals. Many communities have Community Mediation Programs and Court Mediation Programs. You want to know how long the mediator has been practicing and what training he or she has had. Anyone can hang out his shingle and say he is a mediator, so do your homework and make sure the person you select is experienced, knowledgeable, and comes recommended by others.

### *Case in Point—Sam and Marilyn* (bad case for mediation)

*Sam and Marilyn were married for 23 years. They had three children, ages 20, 17, and 13. I received a call from Marilyn's therapist asking whether I could see Marilyn as soon as possible, as Marilyn and Sam had been meeting with a mediator and the therapist wanted me to go over the proposed agreement with Marilyn before she signed anything.*

*Marilyn called me to make an appointment. She said she had a mediation session scheduled for that evening. I told her not to sign anything until we had a chance to meet and go over the agreement together. When Marilyn came in for the appointment she had already signed the agreement. It didn't take long for me to see she had signed a bad agreement, giving up much more than she should have under the circumstances, including custody of her son.*

*Marilyn had not worked outside the home during the marriage except for an occasional part-time job. Sam was the breadwinner and wanted Marilyn at home to take care of the children and to take care of him. He wanted dinner on the table at the same time every night, he wanted the house kept clean, and he wanted sex when he wanted sex. For 20 years she had lived in this controlling situation. Finally, she reached her limit (and everyone has one) with the way he treated her and said, "I've had enough." Unfortunately, she didn't seek out the professional help she needed to end the marriage in a way that was fair to her and that would adequately compensate her for the long marriage soon enough. Under the agreement, she received no spousal support, only thirty percent of the marital estate, and she gave up custody of her youngest son. The oldest child was already living on her own and the middle child was heading off to college.*

*When I asked Marilyn why she had signed the agreement before we had a chance to meet and review it, she said she just wanted to get Sam to leave her alone. He had been badgering her to sign the agreement, and she was simply worn out. After years of being yelled at, pushed around, belittled, and controlled, she just wanted him to go away. I understood this, but the result for her was a very bad agreement that left her with few financial resources for her future.*

*Additionally, she had agreed for her youngest son to continue to live in the home with Sam, while she had to move out. This was devastating to her as she had been the primary caretaker of the children and quickly realized that Sam's agenda was to turn the boys against her. He was somewhat successful in this endeavor. We spent the next three years in court litigating custody and visitation and having to force Sam to allow Marilyn to see her younger son.*

*Marilyn's financial life was a mess. She had inadequate funds to support herself. The only jobs she was able to get paid minimum wage. Suddenly life became incredibly difficult for her on many levels. She never regretted leaving the marriage, but she did regret the way it happened. Marilyn had a good therapist and was receiving emotional and psychological support, but she needed a trusted legal advisor as well.*

*This is an example of how bad a case can get when there is an imbalance of power in the relationship and a history of emotional or physical abuse. This was not an appropriate case for mediation. Because of Sam's bullying nature, Marilyn would have done much better with a good collaborative lawyer or even by pursuing litigation.*

### *Case in Point—Charles and Cathy* (good case for mediation)

*Cathy came to see me wanting information about a collaborative divorce. She had heard about the collaborative process and thought it would be a good way for her and her husband to work out the division of their property.*

*She and her husband, Charles, had been living separately for over a year. They had one child together who had just turned 18. Cathy was in a relationship with another man and was anxious to proceed with a divorce. She had been honest with Charles about the relationship. He didn't want the divorce and was reluctant to discuss it with her at all.*

*I explained the different process choices to Cathy, and she asked me to send Charles a letter explaining the collaborative process, which I did.*

*Charles was not responsive to Cathy's request about collaboration, except to say that he didn't want to go to a lawyer at all. I didn't hear from her for several months. During that time, they had some conversations about how they would divide their assets. Since Charles did not want to hire a lawyer, Cathy agreed to go to a mediator. They met with the mediator two times and were able to come to an agreement on everything. The mediator prepared an agreement and sent it to both of them to review.*

*Cathy and I met to review the agreement. After making a few changes, they both signed off on it and shortly after that, the divorce was finalized.*

*This case is significantly different from the case involving Sam and Marilyn. When Cathy first came to see me, she and Charles were in very different places in the Emotional Divorce. I didn't hear from Cathy for several months. What she really did during this time was to give Charles time to catch up with her emotionally so he was able to meet with her and make decisions about their assets. If she had pushed this to happen on "her time," it might have turned into a very different case. Her ability to be respectful and patient with him made all the difference. They probably would have ended up with the same division of property in collaboration or even litigation, but their relationship would not have survived as it did, nor would their daughter be thriving as she is now.*

*This is an excellent example of clients maintaining control of their own case, saving money, and working through their conflict on their own time schedule.*

## OPTION FIVE—DO IT YOURSELF

### Do It Yourself at a Glance

- Ultimate in terms of privacy and control

- Pace of case determined by clients

- Case resolves without lawyers or court

- Best when clients communicate well and agree on what they want

- Allows clients to have an ongoing relationship

### The Details

Some people are able to do their own divorces, without the involvement of lawyers. This is the least intrusive way to resolve your issues—you and your spouse sit down and reach your own agreement on important matters, such as child custody arrangements, support, and property division.

Some couples are able to resolve all their issues without any professional assistance at all, from writing up their own property settlement agreement to finalizing the divorce through the court system. This option works best when you and your spouse have mutually agreed to separate and divorce, you have a trusting relationship, and one or both of you is familiar with the legal system and the divorce process.

If you are not completely comfortable with doing it yourself and want to make sure you are complying with all the legal nuances of your jurisdiction, you can always go to a lawyer just for a consultation to review what you and your spouse have agreed to. Be advised, though, that a lawyer *cannot* represent both of you.

Frequently, people call me to review their agreement to make sure everything is in order. I review the proposed agreement and make suggestions as needed, and then advise the client to have his or her spouse take the agreement to another lawyer for a consultation as well. This process of using a lawyer on an "as needed" basis is sometimes called "unbundling." This is a smart thing to do if either you or your spouse is not completely comfortable with proceeding on your own. Ultimately, you want an agreement and a final divorce that is complete and correct for you, and one that won't cause problems for either of you down the road.

### *Case in Point—Hank and Susan*

*Hank and Susan had been married for almost 40 years. They had grown children and a couple of grandchildren. Hank was in his 60s and retired from a successful career. He was healthy and happily enjoying himself in retirement. Divorce was the last thing he thought would ever happen to him.*

*Hank was unaware that Susan had been having an affair for a number of years. When the story came to light, he was in shock, but was willing to continue the marriage. Susan said that was something she could not do. At that point, Hank and Susan agreed that a divorce was their only option. Although Hank was clearly upset about the situation, it was also clear that both of them wanted to remain as friendly as possible.*

*Hank called to make an appointment for a consultation. During that first meeting, he made it clear he had no love for lawyers or judges or the courtroom. He said he and Susan knew what they wanted to do, and they just needed to know how to do it right. Because they had children, grandchildren, and many extended family members, they saw the value in keeping a lid on their emotions and working through things on their own.*

*This is what I call the "Do It Yourself" agreement, whether you write it up yourself or come up with your agreement together and hire a lawyer to do the actual drafting of the settlement agreement. Within a few weeks an agreement was drafted, I reviewed and revised it, and then Hank and Susan signed it. Susan had already purchased a small house and moved out, with Hank's help. When the date came when the divorce could be filed, Hank called me again to finalize the divorce. I filed the paperwork, Susan met with me and signed the necessary documents acknowledging receipt of the documents, and their divorce was final within a week.*

*This is the ultimate example of maintaining control of your case as well as your privacy. Hank and Susan's property settlement and divorce were accomplished exactly as they wanted it, in record time, at minimal cost, and with minimum stress.*

# 9

# MORE ON
# COLLABORATIVE DIVORCE—
# THE KINDER, GENTLER CHOICE

Collaborative Divorce is referred to as the *kinder, gentler* way to divorce. Those words and *divorce* may not feel like a fit for you, but stay with me on this. This chapter will give you more detailed information on how it works.

If you and your spouse decide that the collaborative process is the best option for you, your next step is to hire your collaborative lawyer and other team members as needed. What you will find is a group of professionals who are thrilled you have chosen this process. You may not know or understand the benefits yet, but they do. They are excited to be part of the team that will help you navigate your divorce in a way that allows you to maintain your dignity and integrity, while you are actually learning new and better ways of communicating with your spouse. You will find that you, your spouse, and your children, are all supported in ways that are simply not possible in any other divorce process. I think this concept is hard for many to grasp until they are actually in it, but this truly is the "kinder, gentler way."

If I've piqued your interest about collaborative divorce and you want to know more about how it works, here are answers to the questions I am most often asked. If you don't find the answers to your questions here, please feel free to send me an email and I will respond. You can contact me through my website at www.GracefulDivorceSolutions.com.

## WHAT IS COLLABORATIVE PRACTICE?

Collaborative Practice is the newest divorce dispute-resolution process. The key difference between collaborative practice and conventional divorce is the clients' pledge to reach an agreement without going to court. It's a *client-centered* and *client-controlled* process that focuses on interest-based negotiation rather than the traditional positional bargaining process.

The goal of collaboration is to develop respectful relationships, solve problems together, and prevent a battle in court. In order to accomplish this, the parties agree in writing that they *will not* go to court. **This agreement is what makes the process work.** No one may go to court or even threaten to do so. If that occurs, the process terminates and both collaborative lawyers are disqualified from further involvement in the case.

**Hallmarks of the practice are:**

1. **The focus is on settlement and the future.**

2. **Court is not an option.**

3. **It's a "transparent" process—there is full and complete disclosure by the clients, and the attorneys give their advice and experience in the presence of everyone during all meetings.**

## WHAT IS THE COLLABORATIVE DIVORCE TEAM?

This is an emerging field of collaborative practice, which provides a collaborative divorce team consisting of two lawyers, one or two divorce coaches, a child specialist and a financial specialist to help the couple. Believe it or not, this team of five or six can be more cost effective than the conventional method of divorce.

Keep in mind that divorce affects couples on multiple levels. Remember Chapter Seven and the Four Divorces? Divorce is a complex event involving legal, financial, social, and emotional considerations. When children are involved, there are the additional needs of developing appropriate parenting plans and learning communication skills so the couple can effectively co-parent their children.

In the conventional way of divorcing, lawyers have handled all of these tasks. But since lawyers are not therapists, or accountants, or child specialists, many issues remain unresolved when the divorce is final. Because these issues are not resolved at the time of the legal divorce, they often continue to be litigated and re-litigated for years.

Let me illustrate this concept with Couple A and Couple B. Couple A decided to use the collaborative process. With the help of their team, they were able to come up with a parenting plan that works for them, to agree on child support, and then to proceed to work out the division of their property and the payment of spousal support. Each person got some of what he or she wanted, but not everything. Ultimately, the agreement reached was "acceptable" to both of them. It wasn't perfect, but they could live with it. Also, both felt they had a chance to have their say and to be heard by their spouse about what they needed, what they wanted, and why it was important to them. With the help of their team, they had both achieved a level of empathy for the other, meaning they had been able to put themselves in the other's shoes and see the situation from the perspective of their spouse. So they ended the collaborative process with an acceptable agreement and a respectful relationship.

Contrast that scenario with that of Couple B. Couple B went the conventional divorce route. They hired lawyers who tried to negotiate a settlement, but each side perceived the other as trying to get more than that person's fair share, including time with the children. Neither side understood or even cared about what the other needed or wanted, including the lawyers. The case ended up in court with the judge deciding everything. Neither side was happy with his rulings, especially about the custody and support. Can you see how this case is likely to be litigated for years to come? As long as they have money to pay lawyers, both sides will continue going to court until they get the result they want.

The Collaborative Divorce Team model uses a collaborative team to help the couple on all levels with one goal in mind: to maximize the benefit to the family. The goal is to help more people through the process like Couple A and to eliminate the disaster that happened to Couple B.

## WHO ARE THE COLLABORATIVE TEAM MEMBERS AND WHAT ARE THEIR ROLES?

- **Collaborative Attorney**: has specialized training in the collaborative process and interest-based negotiation, serves to educate the client through the process, advocates for the client, provides legal advice, and helps the client to generate and evaluate options for resolution.

- **Divorce Coach**: a licensed mental health professional with specialized training in collaborative practice who helps the clients and the collaborative professionals to communicate effectively within the process. This person does not act as a therapist in the process but rather helps to manage emotional and psychological issues so the process can move along smoothly. (The licensing qualifications are required by the International Association of Collaborative Professionals. There are many Divorce Coaches and Pre-Divorce Coaches who are very effective in working with clients, but who do not participate in collaborative cases.)

- **Child Specialist**: a licensed mental health professional with specific training in family systems and child development. This person helps the parents and the professionals involved to stay focused on the needs and feelings of any children involved, and to develop an effective co-parenting plan.

- **Financial Counselor**: a neutral financial specialist who helps clients to gather, organize, value, and understand their financial information and to clarify their financial interests and goals. This person is a certified financial planner, chartered financial consultant, certified divorce planner or certified public accountant, with additional training in divorce and family law issues.

## WHY IS THE COLLABORATIVE DIVORCE PROCESS ONE OF THE BEST METHODS TO RESOLVE A DIVORCE?

The collaborative process helps the clients to come up with their own marital separation agreement that is specific to their needs and concerns. The result they achieve in this process is more creative than anything they would achieve in an adversarial process, and it addresses and meets the needs of *both* parties. In this process, the clients and the lawyers take a reasonable approach to all issues. Where there is not agreement, all parties use their best efforts to brainstorm options and proposals that would meet the fundamental needs as expressed by each party. Ultimately, there is compromise on both sides and an acceptable solution is found.

## HOW IS COLLABORATIVE DIVORCE DIFFERENT FROM MEDIATION?

In mediation, there is one neutral professional who meets with the parties to help reach resolution. The mediator *may not* give either party legal advice and cannot help either side advocate his or her position. This can be difficult when there is an imbalance of power between the parties. If one side or the other becomes stubborn, unreasonable, or emotionally upset, the process can become unbalanced. If the mediator tries to assist one party or the other when this happens, he or she may be seen as aligning with that party, whether or not it's true. This can result in either a breakdown in the process or an unbalanced, unfair agreement. Collaborative practice was devised to address these problems. Like mediation, settlement is still the *only agenda* of the process; however, with collaboration, each party has a legal advocate and advisor at all times during the process. For some couples, this levels the playing field and provides opportunity for a balanced and acceptable settlement to both parties.

## HOW IS COLLABORATIVE DIVORCE DIFFERENT FROM DIVORCE LITIGATION?

In collaborative divorce, you and your spouse control the process and make final decisions. In divorce litigation, the judge controls the process and makes the final decisions.

In collaboration, you and your spouse pledge to be respectful and open on all the issues. Litigation is based on an adversarial process and parties tend to try to "hide the ball" in order to gain an advantage.

In collaboration, the costs are manageable and usually less expensive than litigation. In litigation, the costs are unpredictable and can escalate very quickly. The fees you pay to your collaborative lawyer are primarily for time spent *with* your lawyer in the collaborative meetings. The fees you pay to your litigation lawyer are often for hours of time spent by your lawyer reviewing financial documents and preparing for trial.

In collaboration, you and your spouse determine the timetable. The average case can be completed in three to eight months. In litigation, how long your case takes depends on the court system. Because there are usually multiple hearings in litigated cases, they can take one to three years to complete.

In collaboration, your lawyer works with you to achieve a mutually acceptable settlement. In litigation, the lawyers fight to win, which means that someone loses. The truth is there are no winners in litigation. The cost of litigation in terms of time, money, and stress is devastating to both parties, regardless of who "wins."

## WHAT HAPPENS IF ONE SIDE OR THE OTHER HAS A HIDDEN AGENDA OR IS DISHONEST IN SOME WAY?

This can happen. There are never any guarantees with collaboration that both parties will act with integrity. There are also no guarantees of this happening in conventional legal representation. The difference with collaborative law is that a lawyer in this process is *required to withdraw* upon becoming aware that his or her client has not disclosed necessary information, has been dishonest in any way, or is not participating in the process in good faith. This is usually an effective deterrent for most clients to stay true to the process.

Unfortunately, we all know there are dishonest people who will do everything they can to hide assets or conceal money. You're the best judge of your spouse's honesty. If you have confidence in your spouse's basic honesty, then the collaborative process is a good choice for you. If you know your spouse would lie on an income tax return or other financial documents, the collaborative process may not be the best choice for you since that basic honesty would be lacking. You must make the choice that is best for you.

## IS COLLABORATIVE DIVORCE THE BEST CHOICE FOR ME?

It's not for everyone, but Collaborative Divorce is worth considering if some or all of these are true for you:

1. You want a civilized, respectful resolution of your issues.

2. You would like to keep open the possibility of friendship with your partner after the divorce.

3. You and your spouse will be co-parenting children and you want the best co-parenting relationship possible.

4. You want to protect your children from the harm associated with litigated dispute resolution between parents.

5. You and your spouse have friends and extended family in common to whom you both want to remain connected.

6. You have ethical and spiritual beliefs that place high value on taking personal responsibility for handling conflicts with integrity.

7. You value privacy in your personal affairs and do not want details of your problems to be available in the public court record.

8. You value control and autonomous decision-making and do not want to hand over decisions about restructuring your financial and/or child-rearing arrangements to a stranger (i.e., a judge).

9. You recognize the restricted range of outcomes generally available in the public court system, and you want a more creative and customized range of choices available to you and your spouse for resolving your issues.

10. You place as much or more value on the relationships that will exist in your restructured family situation as you place on obtaining the maximum possible amount of money for yourself.

11. You understand that conflict resolution with integrity involves not only achieving your own goals but finding a way to achieve the reasonable goals of the other person.

12. You and your spouse will commit your intelligence and energy toward creative problem solving rather than toward recriminations or revenge—fixing the problem rather than fixing blame.

2001 American Bar Association

## HOW CAN I FIND A COLLABORATIVE LAWYER?

Check out the yellow pages where you live or contact your local bar association for listings of collaborative lawyers. Go to the website for the International Association of Collaborative Professionals (www.collaborativepractice.com) (IACP) to find a listing of collaborative lawyers and practice groups near you. You will find a lot of information on the website about individual practitioners who are members of the IACP, including their backgrounds and training. Make an effort to find the best collaborative practitioners you can. Ask them how many collaborative cases they have handled and how many terminated without agreements. Ask what training they've had in the collaborative process, alternate dispute resolution, and conflict management. Finally, ask family, friends, and other professionals in the community for recommendations and referrals to experienced collaborative practitioners.

The International Association of Collaborative Professionals (IACP) is an international group of lawyers, mental health professionals, and financial professionals who are working together to help clients resolve conflicts. The IACP provides a central resource for training, networking, and implementing standards of practice for collaborative professionals. Be sure to check out the website at www.collaborativepractice.com. There is a wealth of helpful information there, including news articles about collaborative practice and stories about people who chose collaborative divorce. Also, you can download a Collaborative

Divorce Knowledge Kit to help you determine whether this process is right for you.

## IS THE COLLABORATIVE DIVORCE PROCESS EXPENSIVE?

Collaborative lawyers generally charge by the hour, as do conventional family lawyers, and rates vary according to experience. Since every case is different, there's no way to predict cost. It will depend on how simple or complex your issues are, how much time is spent in reaching agreement on each issue, the emotional stages of each of the parties, and whether you and your spouse have already reached many of the agreements. A rule of thumb is that a collaborative case will cost you 50% to 60% of a fully litigated case. It's fair to say that collaboration is the most efficient and economical conflict resolution process for the broadest range of clients, and that litigation is, quite simply, the most expensive way of resolving a dispute.

# 10

# MORE ON LITIGATION—
# THE LEGAL "VORTEX"

The word "vortex" is defined as "a whirling mass of water forming a vacuum at its center, into which anything caught in the motion is drawn; whirlpool." That's what litigation is like. When your case gets caught up in the "whirling mass," it takes on a life of its own. Anything and everything can get caught up in the motion and drawn in. You lose all power and control over where it goes and how it turns out.

Let me make a disclaimer at this point. I realize that sometimes there is no other option but to litigate. Unfortunately, some cases simply cannot be resolved any other way. As I mentioned in Chapter Seven, cases involving domestic violence and/or mental illness often end up in litigation because the parties are simply not able to reach agreement through the other processes available. If these exceptions do not apply to you, but you still find yourself in the middle of a litigated divorce, or if your spouse has initiated a divorce through the courts and you find yourself in the midst of a highly adversarial situation, please understand that this happens.

This book will still be helpful to you in making decisions about your case. You can still be proactive with your attorney and with taking care of yourself and your children, and you can still take the highest road possible under your particular circumstances.

Let's begin by looking at the conventional litigation model. When most people decide to divorce, the first thing they do is hire a lawyer. The lawyer files certain papers (called a "complaint" and "pleadings") in the local courts to initiate the divorce action. If it's a contested case, meaning the parties are not in agreement about issues regarding the children, money, or division of property, these papers will often allege wrongdoing on the part of the other spouse. The lawyer's strategy here is to place his or her client in the best position in preparation for court. In this highly adversarial process, each lawyer's job is to make his or her client look as good as possible and the other client look as bad as possible. The worse the lawyers can make each other's client look, and the more dirt they can dig up on the other person, the better their chances of having the judge rule for their client. If the judge sees it the way of one particular spouse, then that spouse will "win" custody, support, and maybe even more than fifty percent of the marital assets. At least that's the common thought process, but it isn't necessarily what happens.

When one party to a divorce is served with papers like those just described, filled with allegations and accusations, whether true or not, how do you think the person will react? He or she is angry, hurt, astonished, and wants to fight back. The words I hear in my office are "This is unbelievable!" "Who wrote this stuff?" "It's all a lie!" and "Wait 'til I tell you what he/she did to me!"

The job of the lawyer representing the person who just got served is to protect his client. In order to do that, the lawyer will "fire" back with a similar set of papers, likely alleging even worse wrongdoings on the part of the other spouse, all in an attempt to *position* his client to look better to the judge. Notice here how just the *language* used by lawyers sets us up for battle. The judge reads these pleadings before any hearing in the case, so the lawyers often get very creative in what they write. The lawyers don't have to know for a fact that what they are writing is true. They just have to have a "good faith" basis for making the allegation.

I bet by now you're getting the picture. Do you see how quickly this situation can spiral out of control, and how much "collateral damage" (feel like it's war yet?) there can be to the children and family? The current legal system (vortex!) and divorce do not mix. How is it possible that this destructive process can be good for the future of family relationships?

**The legal system is not set up to solve the problems associated with ending a marriage, so why do we keep using it?**

Step back into the scenario above where the case begins to take on a life of its own. Papers are filed and the clients and the lawyers begin to prepare for the first of what may be several court hearings. What happens to the children in this situation? When the parents feel like they are caught up in "the fight of their lives," what are the children experiencing? I can tell you it's an extremely difficult time for the children. They are sad and scared because they don't know what to expect. What's worse is that both parents truly believe what they are doing is best for their children. However, what I often see is that the parents are so caught up in their own emotional pain, they just aren't aware of how their children are being affected.

So, if you are thinking about litigating your divorce, including custody, you might want to think again. A custody battle is rarely, if ever, in the children's best interest. Here are some **reasons why avoiding a custody battle is best for your children:**

- You and your lawyer can't pick the judge.

- Not every judge will deal with your parenting issues the same way.

- Judges don't like custody cases, for obvious reasons. Because of this, they may take the "path of least resistance" rather than a more difficult path that is ultimately better for your children.

- The judge makes decisions about your children and your life, without really knowing you and based on little information. All she knows about you is what she hears from the time you walk into the courtroom until you walk out.

- The judge might not decide conclusively. Instead, she might ask you and your spouse to come back to court later to review how things are going for your children since you were last in court.

- The judge might make a decision totally at odds with your goals. How will you feel if you don't get what you want or the judge doesn't pay attention to evidence you think is important?

- Because of the way the court system operates, and the fact that judges are human, even the best judge can get it "wrong."

In summary, here are **three truths** about litigated divorce:

1. **Neither spouse ever "wins."** Almost all desired victories in litigated cases are empty, expensive, and destructive.

2. **Don't fantasize that a legal battle will get you personal satisfaction or vindication. It seldom happens.** Neither does the legal battle put an end to the parents squabbling, nor does it make better decisions than you and your spouse could have done yourselves.

3. **What does come out of the legal battle is a great deal of harm for the family**—it wrecks the opportunity for parents to learn how to be cooperative, it causes serious damage to the children, and it adversely impacts the family's finances.

Litigation needs to be avoided if at all possible. Instead of going down that familiar road, **stop and change course**—step into a new way of thinking where the first action you take when deciding to divorce is to sit down with your spouse and agree on how to do it. If you aren't able to sit down with your spouse, get someone to help you do so, like a minister, rabbi, therapist, or trusted mutual friend. Think about the Big Picture for your life and make that happen by making thoughtful, responsible, and deliberate choices.

(Again, if you are one who doesn't like to write in books, and since it's vitally important to this process that you take some time to think about and write out your responses to the following questions, I have provided a blank template of this for you at my website. Visit www.GracefulDivorceSolutions.com/book to download your copy. No excuses now for not doing these exercises!)

## *ASK YOURSELF:*

Is going to court something I really want to do? Explain.

_____

_____

_____

_____

_____

What advantages do I see for my situation?

_____

_____

_____

_____

What disadvantages do I see for my situation?

_____

_____

_____

_____

In what ways would going to court help me achieve my Big Picture?

_____

_____

_____

_____

Am I able to sit down with my spouse and discuss this? If not, who can help me do this?

_____

_____

_____

_____

Who can help me keep my focus on my Big Picture, help me manage my emotions, and help me follow through with my intentions?

_____

_____

_____

_____

Am I willing to seek out those people and use them through my divorce to help make it go better for me?

_____

_____

_____

_____

### _Case in Point—Robert and Mandy_

_Robert and Mandy had been married for four years and had a 2½ year old daughter, Sarah. Robert came to see me after Mandy had gotten a protective order against him alleging physical abuse._

*He was devastated and upset at the allegations made by his wife. Most upsetting to him was that the child's name was on the protective order also. This meant he could not have any contact with his wife or his child until they got into court.*

*When he came to see me, he hadn't seen his daughter in over a week, and it was another week before the court date. He said he helped to care for his daughter every day, he was worried about her, and it was difficult for him not to see her. He also said his wife was having an affair, and he wanted to file a divorce on the grounds of adultery.*

*It was clear that Robert was dealing with a huge range of emotions—fear, anger, hurt, betrayal, and even rage. I asked him questions about his relationship with his daughter and what he wanted his life to look like when the divorce was over. At first he wanted physical custody of Sarah, with Mandy having visitation. Gradually, he came to think it would be best for Sarah to spend significant time with both parents. As upset as Robert was with Mandy, he knew Sarah was attached to both of them and needed frequent contact with both of her parents.*

*Over time, Robert began to get the Big Picture view of his case. He had to decide whether litigation was going to help him get what he wanted. Over the next few months, we had several conversations about how to get the best outcome, and about what would be best for him and for his daughter. We resolved the protective order without litigating, and we reached a temporary agreement on a shared custody schedule. Robert was pleased about that, and his daughter was doing well, but he still felt strongly about pursuing the divorce on the grounds of adultery.*

*My job was to help Robert see the potential impact taking this action would have on what he was telling me he ultimately wanted for himself and Sarah. What was Robert's idea of what would happen? He thought he would get what he wanted, which was satisfaction—people would know that Mandy had cheated on him. His mental image of this scenario felt pretty darn good. He would be vindicated and "people" would see Mandy for who she really was.*

*But what would likely really happen?*

- *Robert would file a divorce on the grounds of adultery, with details about where, when, and with whom, and a court date would be set.*

- *Mandy would counter file on the grounds of cruelty, alleging Robert had been physically and emotionally abusive throughout the marriage, that he had been controlling and jealous, etc. And, by the way, Mandy's lawyer is not available on the court date set, so there is the first of what could be many continuances.*

- *Are the allegations made by each side true? It doesn't matter. What matters is how we have gone from the situation where two parents had agreed to share custody of their child, and were actually doing it successfully, to total escalation because of the statements made by each about the other. Both sides are now angry at the other, and both now want primary custody. The lines in the sand have been drawn. It's war.*

*We now have a full-blown custody fight, with each side painting the ugliest picture of the other. We've gone from a win-win situation to a lose-lose situation. And who loses? The entire family loses, but most of all Sarah. The entire family (including the involved grandparents) would suffer emotionally and financially.*

*This is a powerful picture of how this process could have gone. But Robert was able to avoid this potential disaster when he came to the understanding of how going to court was like "rolling the dice." There was no assurance that his picture of how it would go would be the reality, and he simply wasn't willing to risk the stability that had been established for his daughter for this unknown outcome. This wasn't easy for him because he had such strong feelings; however, over time he was able to let go of that anger, focus on his daughter, and begin to get on with his own life. Ultimately, he achieved an excellent result and was grateful for the time he took to consider his choices.*

# 11

## FALLING OFF THE "EFFECTIVE COMMUNICATION" WAGON—

## WHEN YOUR BEST INTENTIONS JUST DON'T WORK

I can hear you now. All of this sounds great and makes sense, but what about when my spouse has been abusive to me or has addiction issues, and I don't trust him or her, or I'm afraid? Or what about if my spouse has mental health issues, like bipolar disorder or some other personality disorder, and we can have a good conversation one day and the next day everything has changed and it's like we never even had that conversation? Or what about when my spouse and I are really trying to bridge that communication gap, but we keep falling off the "effective communication" wagon and getting into ridiculous and destructive arguments? What about if I feel like I tried and tried, but it just didn't work, and I feel like there's no going back and I just want it over?

These situations happen, and sometimes one spouse's good intentions of taking the highest road possible and reaching an amicable and fair settlement for all just doesn't work. Why? Because the other spouse, for whatever reason, just cannot get on that same road. Taking the highest road possible sounds great in theory and is great when both spouses agree that is what they want and they are able to follow through. They may be moving along at different paces and maybe even in different vehicles at times, but they're still on the same road and will ultimately reach their destination in a way both of them can live with.

So what do you do when you want the best, fairest, and most peaceful resolution possible, but your spouse will not cooperate with that approach? He or she may be anywhere on the spectrum from completely unavailable and avoiding dealing with the situation at all, to having hired the most aggressive litigator in town in order to punish you for wanting out of the marriage. Sure makes it hard to play nice, doesn't it?

**Here are my suggestions for this situation:**

**First, determine, as best you can, where your spouse is on the spectrum.** Is the situation salvageable or not? For example, if the issues of mental health problems, or addiction issues, or domestic violence do not apply to your situation, then is the issue that the two of you are in different places in the Emotional Divorce and you just need to back up and give your spouse time and space to "be" with what's happening in your relationship? Sometimes it's as simple as being patient, respectful, and knowing when to try to have discussions about your situation and when to let it be. The key throughout this is to continue to express yourself honestly and kindly, but firmly and consistently, so as not to confuse your spouse about where you are in the process.

If the issue here is, in fact, the timing and your spouse being in a different place in the Emotional Divorce and needing time to catch up with you, then this approach will serve you well and ultimately will lead to the more amicable and respectful divorce you are seeking. It's the rare case when both spouses are in the same place in the Emotional Divorce, so it makes sense to be sensitive to this possibility and to start here with your evaluation.

Also, put yourself in your spouse's shoes at this very moment. Very often people react the way they do because of some fear that comes up for them. What is he or she most afraid of? Is it about money? Is it about the house and whether it needs to be sold and where everyone will live? Is it about the children and fears about not being able to see them very much? Is it about what other people will think and how to fit in now as a divorced person? All of these thoughts are real and painful and play a role in people's ability to communicate.

If you can practice being empathetic toward your spouse in this way, and you try to understand his or her fears, then you can take steps to address those fears and assure your spouse that what he or she fears is not what you want to see happen either. For example, if your spouse is afraid he or she will not get to see the children very much, be assuring that you have no intentions of withholding the children from him or her and that you want the children to spend lots of time with both of you, because that's what's best for the children. If the issue is money, be assuring that you will work together on this so both of you can move forward in a financially acceptable way. All of this may seem challenging, but if the issue for your spouse is timing and needing time to process and catch up in terms of the Emotional Divorce, I highly recommend this approach. It will take effort on your part, but it will definitely get you where you want to go.

**Second, what if you evaluate your situation and come to the conclusion that, despite your good intentions, your spouse's mental health issues or addiction issues are just too big, and you aren't able to take the high road of your choice, like mediation or collaboration?** If this is your situation, I recommend first that you find a counselor who can meet with the two of you together and help you in your communication and also help you determine whether you will be able to proceed the way you want. If your spouse refuses to get help or refuses to go to counseling, then at least you tried that avenue first. Next, I recommend you hire an attorney who specializes in the area of family law and who is trained in mediation or collaboration, but who is also an effective litigator. Depending on your situation, you need to take steps to protect yourself and your children, if you have children, and to send a message to your spouse that you are moving forward with your decision to divorce.

You can still be honest and kind throughout, as well as firm and consistent in your words and actions. You can still be on the high road of intending to end your marriage in a decent and dignified way. You may have no control over your spouse and what he or she does or says, but you do have control over yourself. Just decide how you want to go through this and stick to it. Do not allow the antics of your mentally ill or unbalanced spouse to take you out of that place of good intention. Do not let the actions or words of this person, who is not thinking with a rational, healthy mind, cause you to do or say anything that would later cause you regret or hurt your case. I know this sounds easier said than done, and it probably is, but just continue to make the effort and keep your center. Try to get back to that Big Picture view of your life.

Again, practice empathy toward your spouse and remember that he or she is not thinking in the same way you are. Remember this person has a mental illness, imbalance, or addiction and is probably doing the best he or she can with the situation. I also highly recommend that you find your own therapist or counselor during this stressful time to help you cope with your specific situation. A therapist will support you, help keep you balanced, and teach you tricks and tools for coping with your spouse and your situation.

**Third is the issue of domestic violence. If you are a victim of domestic violence, then you have no choice but to take steps to protect yourself.** I urge you to get help and to be extremely proactive for yourself. First, learn as much as you can about domestic violence and get clear on how it has been happening to you and in your household. Second, get connected with a therapist who can help you understand the dynamics of domestic violence and the role you played in your relationship. Learn what changes you can make to heal yourself and to set yourself up for future healthy relationships. Third, hire a compassionate and effective lawyer who can walk through this process with you in a supportive way, but also make sure you are being protected in the legal divorce.

After prosecuting domestic violence and sexual assault cases for several years and then practicing family law for several more years, I continue to be amazed at how uninformed people are about domestic violence and how they consider some abusive behaviors normal and acceptable. So what is domestic violence? It's about power and control. It isn't just about hitting or fighting or cussing or being mean. It's more than that. It's about a chronic use and abuse of power, and the abuser will use whatever it takes—threats, intimidation, and physical violence—to get and maintain control of his or her partner.

Domestic violence affects all people in all walks of life. Since a vast majority of cases are never even reported, it's much more prevalent than we can even know. Anyone can be a victim. The violence can take many forms and can happen just occasionally or all the time. It can be emotional, sexual, or physical. Whatever form it takes, it's about one person exerting power and control over another.

Here are some typical behaviors of abusers. They may do one, some, or all of these things to exert and maintain control over you. If you are experiencing any of these, then call it what it is, domestic violence, and get some help:

- **Name-calling or putdowns**—like you're stupid; you're ugly; you can't do anything right; plus all sorts of ugly and vulgar cuss names that I can't print here.

- **Preventing you from contacting your family or friends**—meaning isolating you from the people most important in your life, telling you that your family is trying to break up your relationship, not wanting you to spend time alone with them.

- **Withholding or hiding money**—you can't go anywhere (like leave them!) if you don't have money in your pocket or aren't able to access bank accounts.

- **Preventing you from have getting or keeping a job**—many abusers want you at home and not out with other people in a workplace where you may be attracted to another, or another may be attracted to you.

- **Threatened or actual physical harm**—abusers may threaten and intimidate you with physical harm, yet never actually put their hands on you, or they may push, shove, slap, hit, spit, etc., depending on how much control they feel the need to exert or how much control they feel they are losing over you.

- **Sexual assault**—being forced to engage in sexual activity against your will is domestic violence. No one has a right to your body but you, unless you consent.

- **Stalking**—following you, showing up where you are unexpectedly (giving you the creeps!), listening to your phone calls, tracking you with a device on your car or tapping your phone.

- **Intimidation**—Abusers like to use the fear factor. If you are behaving in a certain way around your partner out of fear of him or her, for whatever reason, then you are being intimidated in some way. Your spouse is controlling your behavior by causing you to be afraid, even though it may be very subtle.

If you find yourself dealing with any of these situations, get some help from qualified professionals about some possible courses of action for you. Once you are able to define clearly the reasons why effective communication is not working for you, then you can make a plan to try to resolve the problem. Once you have a plan in place and take steps that could help to improve your situation, at least you will have taken the highest road possible for you and sent the message that your intentions are to be fair and decent. This can be a difficult balancing act here, to make sure you are protecting your own interests and being proactive on your behalf, and at the same time acting as fairly as possible toward your spouse. Go out and find some trusted, talented, and knowledgeable advisors to help you make the best decisions for your circumstances.

And, finally, please know that there are times, as I have outlined above, when you have no choice but to dig in and take the steps necessary to protect yourself and your children. If, after reviewing your situation and considering your options, you determine this is what you need to do, then by all means do it. I still maintain, even when you have to take aggressive action, that you can do it as kindly and decently as possible.

# 12

# THE FIVE ISSUES OF DIVORCE

Hopefully by now you have zeroed in on which divorce process you would like to use. Regardless of your process choice, there are certain issues that must be dealt with in all divorces. These issues are custody, visitation, child support, property division, and spousal support.

Keep in mind that every state has different laws, so the information here is generic but should be generally applicable wherever you are. Each overview will at least give you the basics and help you begin thinking about your personal situation and begin to outline the steps you will want to take to achieve your overall goals.

While considering these issues, remember to ask yourself these questions once again:

- What do I want my life to look like when my divorce is done?

- What kind of relationship do I want with my spouse when the divorce is done?

- What kind of relationship do I want our children to have with each of us when the divorce is done?

If you don't have children, skip ahead to the sections on Property Division and Spousal Support.

## CUSTODY

Clients usually come to me confused about what the word "custody" means. There are a number of legal terms to understand in order for all of this to make sense—like sole legal custody, joint legal custody, sole physical custody, primary physical custody, joint physical custody, etc. What happens is people sometimes get hung up on the *terminology* without really understanding it, and this lack of understanding can cause unnecessary problems. Once again, this is a place where the legal system has the effect of setting people up for failure. They hear these terms and become aligned with a certain "position" without really understanding them, which can make it harder to reach an agreement.

Obviously custody can be a highly emotional issue for parents. Where children will live and how you will co-parent in two households is complicated. Once parents have an understanding of the legal definitions of custody, they're better able to focus on the best parenting arrangement or schedule for their children. I have found that when the emphasis can be on what the parenting schedule will *look* like and how it will work for the parents and the children, rather than what it's *called* in legal terms, then this is a more productive approach to resolving the custody situation. It's no longer about one parent or the other *getting* something (like physical custody), but now about the schedule and the actual time when the children will be with each parent.

The most important distinction is between *legal* custody and *physical* custody. Legal custody has to do with who makes important decisions about the children, and physical custody has to do with where they live. Most parents have **joint legal custody**, which means that both parents share the responsibility for making important decisions concerning the children. For example, the parents make decisions together regarding where the children go to school, what doctor they go to, what activities they participate in, whether or not they get braces or have surgery, etc.

**Sole legal custody** means one parent only has the responsibility for the care and control of the children and has the authority to make the primary decisions regarding them. Courts will typically order this only when the parents cannot communicate with each other, are unable to make important decisions together regarding the children, or when one parent lives far away and has little contact with the children. For example, if the parents cannot agree on care for the children, such as which school they should go to or what kind of health care they should have, then obviously this is a major issue that affects the children. One of the parents must have authority to make decisions so the children receive the care they need.

**Physical custody** has to do with where the children live. One parent may have primary physical custody, or the parents may have a shared custody arrangement. Shared physical custody arrangements can be as creative as are necessary based on the needs of the children and the schedules of the parents. Children can spend equal time at each parent's home, or any other time division that works for the family.

If the courts are involved in this dispute, a judge will make his or her decision based on a standard called "**the best interests of the child.**" There are a number of factors the judge considers, typically including the following:

- The age and physical and mental condition of the child, as well as the child's changing developmental needs.

- The age and physical and mental condition of each parent.

- The relationship existing between each parent and each child, giving consideration to the positive involvement with the child's life, and the parent's ability to assess accurately and meet the emotional, intellectual, and physical needs of the child.

- The needs of the child, including important relationships of the child, such as those with siblings, peers, and extended family members.

- The role that each parent has played, and will play in the future, in the upbringing and care of the child.

- The tendency of each parent to support actively the child's contact and relationship with the other parent, including whether a parent has unreasonably denied the other parent access to or visitation with the child.

- The willingness and demonstrated ability of each parent to maintain a close and continuing relationship with the child, and the ability of each parent to cooperate in and resolve disputes regarding matters affecting the child.

- The reasonable preference of the child, if the court deems the child to be of reasonable intelligence, understanding, age, and experience to express such a preference.

- Any history of family abuse.

- Other factors the court determines are important.

You will find these or similar "guidelines" for the court in deciding custody in the laws of most states. In his ruling, the judge will go through each of these factors, like a checklist, and will decide whether one or the other parent best meets the needs of the children. He will make his ultimate decision regarding custody based on which parent comes out ahead. "*Other factors the court determines are important*" is language that gives the court a tremendous amount of discretion. This is where it gets scary for clients and hairy for lawyers to try to predict for their clients what a particular judge will do in their case. A case can be somewhat predictable based on the law, but never predictable based on the judge. Judges are human beings, like you, with good days and bad days, and with life experiences and biases, just like all of us. Even when I have what I feel is a strong case for custody, I have to tell my clients that there are no guarantees. It's always a roll of the dice to walk into the courtroom.

## VISITATION

Visitation generally refers to the situation when the children have their primary residence with one parent and "visit" the other. For many parents, the term itself is a hot button, and I advocate not using it. I've had many fathers tell me they have no intention of being an "every other weekend Dad" and "visiting" with their children. It was important to them that they continue to have significant and consistent interaction with their children. For this reason, I prefer not to use the term "visitation" and instead speak of the arrangements in terms of each parent's "time" with the children, the "children's schedule with each parent," the "parenting plan," etc.

The semantics are important. If using different language helps to reduce the emotion of the situation, then we need to use different language. It's that simple. The point is to keep the parents focused on what is best for the children, and to keep the children healthy, happy, and emotionally balanced. If this is their goal (and ninety-nine percent of the time it is the goal for divorcing parents), then why get caught up in what all of it is *called*? By using neutral language, we keep the focus where it needs to be.

If the issue of visitation becomes adversarial and ends up in court, a judge will consider the same factors as listed above in making his or her decision. Again, the judge has a tremendous amount of discretion when making a ruling in this area. So going into court on this is another roll of the dice.

## CHILD SUPPORT

Child support is money paid by one parent to the other to help support the children. This amount is intended to help support all aspects of the child's life, including food, housing, utilities, clothing, incidentals, school-related expenses, etc. The amount of child support paid will depend primarily on the income of the parents and the custody arrangement of the children. Both parents have a legal obligation to provide financial support for their children until the children turn 18 and are legally adults.

**How is the amount of support determined?** Most states have child support guidelines based on a standard calculation. The numbers that go into the calculation include:

- Gross income of each parent

- Work-related child care costs

- Health insurance costs for the children

- Any extraordinary medical or dental expenses (like braces)

- Number of days the children are with each parent

Parents can use the child support guidelines available in their jurisdiction to determine the amount of child support in their situation, or they can agree between themselves on this issue. The beauty of any of the process choices except litigation is that you, the parents, get to decide all these things based on what works best for you and your children. Whatever you agree on is put into your agreement. The more you and your spouse cooperate regarding the financial support and needs of your children, the better your children will do over time. Children suffer when their parents argue about money or when one parent does not fulfill his or her legal obligation to help financially support the children.

Clients often want to know who pays if their children go to college. Both parents have a legal obligation to support their children financially until they turn 18. Once they turn 18, the courts have no authority to order either parent to provide financial support for them, except in cases where a child has ongoing special needs. Most parents do feel a moral obligation to continue to help pay for their children's financial support, however. Also, parents can choose to include in their agreement how they will pay for college. If they include this in their property settlement agreement, then it is legally binding and enforceable on both of them when the time for college arrives.

## IMPORTANT NOTE ON CUSTODY, VISITATION, AND CHILD SUPPORT

Clients often say, "I just want this decided and over with!" This is understandable. It's normal to want certainty and closure in life. However, when it comes to the children, it's never over. It might be settled for the moment, but if circumstances change, either parent can bring the case back into mediation, collaboration, or litigation.

Even though clients don't like hearing this, there is good reason for it. The standard to be observed and what judges are always considering is "the best interests of the children." Over time, "the best interests of the children" may change. The arrangements you have for them today with respect to custody, visitation, and support may not work in another year, or two years, or five years. Because of this, these issues are never set in stone. They are never permanent. Most states have laws that provide for the opportunity to change custody, visitation, or child support any time there is a change of circumstances that would impact the children and affect their best interests.

## PROPERTY DIVISION

The division of property in a divorce can be complicated. The parties need to figure out what they own and what they owe. The difference will be the **marital estate**. Then they need to determine how to divide the marital estate. Problems arise when trying to figure out whether an asset is marital, separate, or hybrid (part marital and part separate). This is called "classification" of the asset. I often spend a lot of time with my clients explaining this and helping them to gather the information necessary to know how to classify their assets.

**Separate property** is classified as:

- Any property acquired before the marriage

- Any property acquired during the marriage by inheritance or from a source other than your spouse that has been kept separate

- Property acquired after the date of separation

**Marital property** is classified as:

- Any property titled in the name of both parties (except possibly re-titled property)

- Any property acquired during the marriage which is not separate property

**Hybrid property** is classified as:

- Any property owned before the marriage that has increased significantly in value during the marriage due to the efforts of either party or the addition of marital property

- Any property acquired by one spouse during the marriage by gift or inheritance which has been combined with marital property (like using an inheritance to pay off the mortgage on the marital home)

**Marital property usually consists of the following**:

- marital home and any other real estate acquired during the marriage

- any joint bank accounts

- investment accounts

- retirement accounts

- 401(k)s and pensions

- motor vehicles

- household furniture and furnishings

- art work

- jewelry

- collectibles

Once these assets are determined, they need to be valued. The value can be an amount the parties mutually agree on or appraisals can be made to determine current fair market value.

**Marital debt usually consists of the following:**

- mortgages on the marital home or other real estate

- credit card debts

- debt obligations on motor vehicles

- any other debt obligations incurred during the marriage

The simplest way to explain the division of property is to say we determine the fair market value of the marital assets, then deduct the amount of marital debt, leaving an amount we call the marital estate, which is the amount to be divided between the parties. The next question is how to divide the property, whether it is an even fifty/fifty split or some other division. Most courts initially assume an equal split; however, based on the evidence and consideration of a number of factors, the court may award a different division, such as 55/45, 60/40, etc.

**The factors taken into consideration by a judge usually include the following:**

- The financial contributions made by each spouse to the marriage (e.g., who made the money, how much, etc.)

- The non-financial contributions made by each (e.g., if one spouse stayed home, raised the children, took care of the home, yard, etc.)

- The length of the marriage

- The ages and physical and mental condition of each spouse

- The reasons for the breakdown of the marriage, including any grounds for divorce (notice how this is just one factor to be considered)

- How and when specific items of marital property were acquired

- The debts and liabilities of each spouse and how and when they were incurred

- The tax consequences to each spouse (e.g., spousal support is deductible on taxes for the paying spouse and income on taxes to the receiving spouse)

- Other factors the court determines are important to consider

Notice again, that catch-all phrase—"other factors the court determines are important to consider." Again, this is where the uncertainty comes in when going to court because we can't predict what a particular judge will do in a particular case on a particular day. As a lawyer who has tried cases in the various courts in my jurisdiction, I can give you the benefit of my experience in similar cases with the same judge, but I still cannot predict what will happen in *your* case.

I have given you a brief explanation of the law as it relates to the division of property. However, if you and your spouse choose a process other than litigation, you are free to come to any resolution that works for you regardless of what the law says. The law can be used for guidance as needed, but if you are outside of litigation, you and your spouse can get as creative as you like in dividing your assets.

## SPOUSAL SUPPORT

Spousal support is money paid by one spouse for the support of the other. In some jurisdictions, it's based on a guideline calculation similar to that done for child support. In other jurisdictions, it's based on one spouse's *ability to pay* support and the other spouse's *need* for it. So if one spouse can show a need to receive support, but the other spouse does not have the ability to pay any support, then no support will be ordered by a court. Likewise, if one spouse has the ability to pay support but the other cannot show a need for it, no support will be ordered by a court. The best way to see whether there is a need and/ or an ability to pay is to have both spouses complete detailed income and expense budget sheets. Having this information is helpful to the clients in coming to an acceptable agreement. If an agreement is not reached, this information is used in court by each side to argue his or her case.

Again, when this matter is handled outside of litigation, the parties are free to create whatever arrangement works best for them. They can agree to a certain amount for a specific period of time. They can change the amount over time. They can agree to a lump sum amount in lieu of monthly support. They can agree for the support to be taxable or non-taxable, deductible or non-deductible. In short, the clients have complete control when they are outside of litigation.

Spousal support is often an emotional issue between the parties. As in child support, both spouses have a legal obligation to maximize their individual incomes for the benefit of themselves and their children. For example, if you decide to quit your job or take a lesser paying job in order to avoid paying either child support or spousal support, it won't work. The court may very well impute income to you based on what you are able to make or the amount you were making at the higher paying job. I've seen people get into big financial trouble by trying to go around the system or their spouse. If this issue is litigated, the courts will "hold your feet to the fire," so to speak, and make you accountable for earning income at your highest potential.

When the case is litigated, the court will also consider a number of factors concerning spousal support. Notice that they are similar to the factors considered by the court when determining division of property. The factors are:

- The obligations, needs, and financial resources of the parties, including income from all pension, profit sharing, or retirement plans

- The standard of living established during the marriage

- The duration of the marriage

- The age and physical and mental condition of the parties and any special circumstances of the family

- The extent to which the age, physical or mental condition, or special circumstances of any child of the parties would make it appropriate that a party not seek employment outside of the home

- The contributions, monetary and nonmonetary, of each party to the well-being of the family

- The property interests of the parties—personal property and real estate

- The provisions regarding the division of the marital property

- The earning capacity, including the skills, education, and training of the parties and the present employment opportunities for each

- The opportunity for, ability of, and the time and costs involved for a party to get the education and training that would help to increase his or her earning ability

- The decisions regarding employment, career, education, and parenting arrangements made by the parties during the marriage and what effect these decisions had on their present and future earning potential

- Such other factors as are necessary to consider the equities between the parties

The importance of many of these factors was discussed in Chapter Three. You may wish to review that chapter as it relates to the payment of spousal support and the factors that are considered when deciding whether support will be paid, and if so, the amount. As you can see, there is a lot to be taken into consideration. Basically, both parties have a responsibility to maximize their incomes to the best of their abilities, and both also have a right to be able to continue in the lifestyle established during the marriage, as much as is feasible under the circumstances. Unfortunately, what I see all too often is that there just isn't enough money for that to be possible and both parties experience a lower living standard after the divorce. The saying, "Two can live cheaper than one" is very true!

So these are the five areas to be addressed in your divorce. The process you choose will dictate how each of these issues is resolved. Choosing a process that allows you more control over your case means you and your spouse can resolve these issues on your terms and at your own pace. When you're not able to reach an agreement and have to go to court, then the judge has discretion to decide. You have the power to control who determines your future.

# 13

# CHOOSING A LAWYER
## GETTING THE RIGHT FIT FOR YOU

One of the most important decisions you'll make when going through your divorce is whether to use a lawyer, and if so, whom to hire. The lawyer you choose can make a big difference in how your case goes. Some lawyers are very collaborative and good at settlement, and others are good at litigating. Some lawyers have more experience than others in family law practice. Some have been practicing for many years and have what I call the "old school" approach to representing people in divorce (prepare to litigate!), and others refuse to do anything but collaborative cases.

Ultimately, the decision you make about your divorce process should impact the lawyer you hire to help you. And if you are on the fence about pursuing a divorce, having a consultation with an experienced divorce lawyer will help you understand the process, the costs, and the possible outcomes. It's important to find someone who is experienced in family law. Would you ask your family doctor to operate on your heart? Probably not. Even though he likely knows about cardiac surgery, he doesn't have the expertise to do heart surgery. It's the same with your divorce. Your divorce is important, and how it goes will significantly affect your future. You want someone who knows the tricks of the trade.

It's also important when choosing a lawyer that you feel there is a good fit. You should feel a connection and a mutual understanding with the lawyer you hire. Just like picking your physician, dentist, or therapist, or even your church, you want to make sure you choose the one who *feels* right to you. If you aren't feeling a connection, don't hesitate to seek a second or even third consultation with other lawyers. Regardless of the process you choose, getting divorced is a very difficult and personal experience, so your lawyer should be someone you trust. He or she is your partner through this process. You need to have faith in his or her ability to help you get to where you want to be.

The key to getting the right lawyer for you is finding someone you can trust, rely on, and who will be your advocate, regardless of the process you are using. That being said, here are four tips to consider when deciding on the best lawyer for you:

1. **Fees**. Lawyer's fees aren't cheap, but the lawyer's hourly rate should not be the determining factor for you. A

higher priced lawyer does not necessarily equal better results. Some people think if something costs more, it must be better. That is not necessarily the case here. Be sure to factor in the rest of these tips along with the costs of a particular lawyer before making your decision.

2. **Experience**. You want to find a lawyer who specializes in the area of family law, or who at least has a practice made up of 50 percent family law cases. Why does this matter? As I stated earlier, family law is a different animal. An experienced divorce lawyer will know the tendencies of the various judges in your jurisdiction and will have worked with the other divorce lawyers in your area, and this will definitely be to your advantage. A lawyer with expertise in family law will also be able to offer you clear explanations of your process choices and be able to answer your burning questions in a way that will make sense to you.

3. **Referrals**. When you open up the phone book to look for a lawyer, you'll be faced with so many ads for divorce lawyers you'll have no idea whom to call. The best way to find a divorce lawyer is to get a recommendation from another professional, like a therapist, financial specialist, or physician, or from another person who has used this lawyer in his or her own divorce. Don't be afraid to ask around. Hearing what others have to say will help you decide whether this is the right lawyer for you.

4. **Good Fit and Accessibility Factor**. It's extremely important that you have a good connection with your lawyer, that you feel comfortable talking to him, and that you are confident in his abilities. It's also extremely important that your lawyer is accessible and responsive to your phone calls, emails, and requests. When first meeting or interviewing lawyers, be sure to ask them about their policies on returning phone calls and emails. Most divorce lawyers try to be responsive to their clients and return calls or emails within 24 hours. On the other hand, be mindful that the lawyer's job is to help you through the divorce process and not to be a therapist to you. Since your lawyer charges for his time, you'll save money if you provide all information to him as requested and communicate your thoughts and feelings clearly and consistently.

Clients sometimes come to me who are already represented by another lawyer but feel like that lawyer isn't doing a good job for them and they don't know what to do. There are warning signs that your lawyer may not be doing the best for you. For example, is he following the plan of action that was set out at the beginning of your case? Is he keeping in touch with you and keeping you informed as to the status of your case? Is he returning your phone calls or emails in a timely manner? Is he billing you appropriately? Is he prepared for your meetings or hearings?

If your answer is "No" to any of these questions, then you may want to consider changing lawyers. If this happens to you, don't feel bad about it. It happens. The key is to open your eyes, pay attention, and make a change when you see these signs. It doesn't make any sense to stay on that path with that lawyer if you are not being represented in the way you want. If you are not able to communicate effectively with your lawyer, seek out someone else.

Likewise, be careful not to have unrealistic expectations of your lawyer. Lawyers are not therapists, although experienced divorce lawyers can be effective at helping clients to manage their emotions during this time. But using your lawyer as a therapist will be expensive for you and may eventually cause your lawyer to avoid your phone calls, emails, and your case. If you become a pest, your lawyer will dread working with you. The best way to document non-emergency incidents with your spouse is to write them down and fax or email them to your lawyer. Do not pick up the phone and call him or her every time something happens. Every time you talk to him on the phone, there will be a charge.

Calmly gathering information and providing it to your lawyer in an organized manner will definitely help save you money. Your lawyer will also respect you and enjoy working with you more. Remember, this relationship should be like a partnership. You are working together to achieve the best resolution for you. Mutual respect, understanding, and clear communication will make this a reality.

Here are some statements that might be helpful as you look for the right lawyer for you. If the lawyer you meet with makes any of the following statements, you should see red flags all over the place and run. Just say "Thank you for your time," and move on to someone else:

- "We're going to win this case. Don't worry about a thing."

- "Under no circumstances leave the home. I don't care about the turmoil, you can't jeopardize your claim to the house."

- "Don't worry about the cost; I'll get it from your ex."

- "We'll ask for the moon in negotiations and then come down a little at a time."

- "Make a list of the worst things your spouse ever did. Memorize it."

- "Listen, those kids belong to you when the order says so; screw your ex's special plans."

- "You can't go to counseling or mediation with your spouse; it could hurt your case."

- "We'll have the kids tell the judge where they want to live."

- "You poor thing. I will take care of all of this for you."

If you hear any of the above statements in your consultation meeting, beware! This person is making promises he or she cannot keep, and it's a clear indication that your case will be one of those that gets sucked into the "legal vortex." You can be assured it will be long, ugly, and expensive. Don't go there!

# 14

# MY CLOSING ARGUMENT— MAKE WAY FOR CHANGE

In closing, I urge you to take the information you find helpful here, what you find to be true for you, and leave the rest. Everyone's path is different, and, as I've said throughout this book, there is no "one size fits all." Your job is to figure out the best way through this for you and your spouse. If you have children, you also want the best resolution for them. If change is happening in your life, make it have the most wonderful and positive meaning possible. There are always valuable lessons in change. I urge you to pay attention and not miss them.

**Here are five thoughts I want to leave with you.**

1. **Divorce is not the end of your world.** For many people, it's the beginning of becoming who they really are. It's a time of growing up, accepting responsibility, and tuning

into who they are as individuals, often for the first time in their lives.

2. **Divorce can (ultimately) be a very positive experience for you.** Usually it takes time to realize this, of course, but here are some examples of positive impacts which former clients have reported to me:

a. Jason got into therapy and came to an understanding of what happened in his relationship, which meant he would not be a repeat relationship offender. Hooray! Too often people jump into new relationships without understanding and dealing with what happened in their former relationships. Too often the patterns continue and they become serial divorcers.

b. Paula gave herself time to heal, spent time understanding herself and her relationship needs, and has now found new, healthier relationships. She is thriving, happier, and more secure than ever.

c. Julia became knowledgeable and proactive about handling finances and will never be financially dependent on another person.

d. Angela, who said she was terrified of being "alone," discovered that she enjoyed her own company, and that discovery has allowed a creativity to emerge that she didn't even know was there. She described this as feeling like she has become a new, more complete, person.

e. Mark learned he could put aside his own pain and focus on the needs of his children. He realized that behaving like an adult and a good parent felt infinitely better than dwelling on the anger and pain on which he had been focused for such a long time.

f. And the stories go on and on.

3. **Learning to keep in mind the Big Picture for you is a habit that will serve you well throughout life to help you keep focused, on track, and in balance.** Remember, the Big Picture means keeping focused on what you want your life to look like next month, next year, and in five or ten years. The actions you take today will help you to make that picture a reality in the future.

4. **Getting divorced gives you the unique opportunity to step into your own power and to realize your wholeness as an individual.** I've watched some people embrace this opportunity, and others run from it. It's your journey and you get to choose which way you go.

5. **The opportunity for growth from divorce is astonishing. It's your choice whether you view your experience as positive or negative.** Whether or not you view your divorce as the best thing that ever happened to you, the worst thing that ever happened to you, or just the thing that happened to you that caused you the most growth, it's all up to you.

I work with my clients from the minute they walk into my office, first to help them decide the best process choice for them, and then to educate them gently about everything I have written about in this book. I hope it has been helpful to you and has caused you to think differently about divorce, and hopefully, to make the best choices for you if you are going through a divorce.

Remember, the way people *do* things is a direct result of the way people *think* about things. My challenge to you is to think differently about divorce. Change your thinking. Decide for yourself that it will be a peaceful process, that you will stay in your integrity, and that you will do what is best for you and your family in the process. Decide that you will learn whatever lessons are there for you from this experience. Put a different picture in your head for yourself, and have a better divorce. Be an example. Be part of the change, an agent of change if you will, and not someone who follows what everyone else is doing or has done in the past. Be intentional—for yourself, your spouse, and your children. Find out for yourself how amazingly good it feels to do so.

And now, I rest my case. I object to the conventional way we do divorce, and so should you! The system is not just flawed. There's not just a little crack there. It's totally busted. It is so senseless and out of control, it's hard for me even to find strong enough words to express this truth.

*wow*
*matches my hope*

But this truth I can express: only you, the person going through it, can make a difference in your own divorce. Take charge of yourself. Become aware of your options. Get good advice from experienced professionals, and then listen to your own inner voice and do what is right for you. If people going through divorce will demand that the system be changed, *then* perhaps more lawyers and legislatures will listen and implement change.

I wonder what would happen if litigation were not an option at all. What if collaboration were the only option? Suppose we took litigation out of the picture and people who could not otherwise agree did not have the option of going before a judge? Do you think we might be able to get creative and figure out new, constructive, positive ways to reach resolution?

I don't know the answer...yet. But I know there is one.

One last thing. If this book has been helpful to you in any way, if it's helped get you going in the right direction for you, if you've made notes in it or highlighted any sections, would you do something for me? Please give this copy to someone else who needs this information. We all know people who are divorcing. Ask them to read it. It will make a difference for them. And over time it will make a huge difference, because over time, we'll reach the proverbial tipping point, and profound change will finally occur in how people resolve conflict and divorce.

Help me spread the word.

Thanks. And Good Luck to You!

# RECOMMENDED READING
# AND RESOURCES

1. Ahrons, Constance, Ph.D. *The Good Divorce: Keeping Your Family Together When Your Marriage Comes Apart.* Harper Collins, 1994.

2. Ahrons, Constance, Ph.D. *We're Still Family: What Grown Children Have to Say About Their Parents' Divorce.* Harper Collins, 2004.

3. Allison, Susan. *Conscious Divorce: Ending a Marriage With Integrity.* Three Rivers Press, 2001.

4. Applewhite, Ashton. *Cutting Loose: Why Women Who End Their Marriages Do So Well.* Harper Collins, 1997.

5. Ellis, Carolyn. *The 7 Pitfalls of Single Parenting: What to Avoid to Help Your Children Thrive After Divorce,* iUniverse, 2007.

6. Ellis, Carolyn. *The Divorce Resource Kit,* available at www.ThriveAfterDivorce.com

7. Fagerstrom, Karen, Milton Kalish, A. Rodney Nurse, and Nancy J. Ross. *Divorce: A Problem to be Solved, Not a Battle to be Fought.* Brookwood Publishing, 1997.

8. Fisher, Roger and William Ury. *Getting To Yes: Negotiating Agreement Without Giving In.* Penguin Books, 1991.

9. Ford, Debbie. *Spiritual Divorce: Divorce as a Catalyst for an Extraordinary Life.* Harper Collins, 2001.

10. Margulies, Sam, Ph.D., J.D. *Getting Divorced Without Ruining Your Life.* Simon and Schuster, 2001.

11. Ricci, Isolina. *Mom's House, Dad's House.* McMillan, 1980.

12. Richardson, Cheryl. *The Art of Extreme Self-Care: Transform Your Life One Month at a Time.* Hay House, 2009.

13. Richardson, Cheryl. *The Unmistakable Touch of Grace: How to Recognize and Respond to the Spiritual Signposts in Your Life.* Simon and Schuster, 2005.

14. Sherman, Ed. *Divorce Solutions: How to Make Any Divorce Better.* Nolo Press, 2003.

15.  Stone, Douglas, Bruce Patton, and Sheila Heen. *Difficult Conversations: How to Discuss What Matters Most.* Penguin Books, 1999.

16.  Stoner, Katherine E. *Divorce Without Court: A Guide to Mediation & Collaborative Divorce.* Nolo Press, 2006.

17.  Tesler, Pauline H., M.A., J.D. and Peggy Thompson, Ph.D. *Collaborative Divorce: The Revolutionary New Way to Restructure Your Family, Resolve Legal Issues, and Move on with Your Life.* Harper Collins, 2006.

18.  Trafford, Abigail. *Crazy Time: Surviving Divorce and Building a New Life.* Harper Collins, 1992.

19.  Wallerstein, Judith S. and Sandra Blakeslee. *What About the Kids? Raising Your Children Before, During, and After Divorce.* Hyperion, 2003.

20.  Webb, Stuart G. and Ronald D. Ousky. *The Collaborative Way to Divorce: The Revolutionary Method That Results in Less Stress, Lower Costs, and Happier Kids—Without Going to Court.* Hudson Street Press, 2006.

# GLOSSARY

**Alimony**:  Payments made to a separated or divorced spouse as required by a divorce decree or separation agreement. Also called spousal support or maintenance.

**Alternate Dispute Resolutions (ADR)**:  Ways of making decisions and resolving disputes other than litigation; includes mediation, collaborative practice, arbitration, and negotiation.

**Child Specialist**:  An experienced, licensed therapist with specific training in the area of family systems, expected behaviors, stages, challenges, and tasks of the development of a child. Child Specialists work with children regarding specific emotional and day-to-day needs as they relate to the divorce process. The Child Specialist works with the parents through the collaborative process in designing a parenting plan that specifically addresses the defined needs of the children as they go through the restructuring of the family.

**Child Support**:  A set amount of money paid by one parent to the other to help support their children after divorce. The amount can be determined by the court or by agreement of the parents and is based on the gross income of each parent.

**Collaborative Attorney**:  An attorney trained in the practice of collaborative practice to help a couple go through their divorce. The attorney addresses the legal issues that a couple faces in a divorce. Through problem-solving negotiations that do not include adversarial techniques (no court), the attorney advises the clients about the law and its effect on them and helps them reach an acceptable agreement.

**Collaborative Divorce**:  Based on collaborative practice principles and the commitment to resolve all disputes out of court.

**Collaborative Law**:  This term describes the legal component of Collaborative Practice, which is made up of the spouses or parties and their attorneys. It consists of two clients and their attorneys working together toward the goal of reaching an efficient, fair, and comprehensive settlement on all of their issues. All negotiations take place in four-way settlement meetings that both clients and attorneys attend. The lawyers cannot go to court or threaten to go to court. Settlement is the only agenda. If either client goes to court, both collaborative lawyers are disqualified from further participation. Each client has built-in legal advice and advocacy during negotiations, and each lawyer's job includes guiding the client toward reasonable resolutions. The legal advice is an integral part of the process, but the clients make all the decisions. The lawyers prepare and process all papers required for the divorce.

**Collaborative Team**:  A Collaborative Team is the group of professionals chosen by the spouses to work with them to resolve their dispute. It can be simply the couple and the collaborative lawyers, or it can also include a neutral financial professional (financial counselor), a divorce coach, a child specialist, or other specialists the couple feels would be helpful. The collaborative team guides and supports the couple as problem solvers, not as adversaries.

**Contested Divorce**:  One in which the husband and wife cannot agree on one or several issues related to the ending of their marriage. When the partners cannot come to an agreement, they must take their issues to a court to be decided.

**Conventional Divorce**:  One in which the parties rely upon the court system and judges to resolve their disputes. Unfortunately, in a conventional divorce, spouses often come to view each other as adversaries, and the divorce may be a battleground. The resulting conflicts can take an immense toll on the family, emotionally and financially.

**Divorce**: A legislatively created and judicially administered process that legally terminates a marriage; also known as dissolution of marriage.

**Divorce Coach**: A skilled professional who is trained to manage a variety of emotions and issues that arise during divorce; Collaborative Divorce Coaches are all licensed mental health professionals (e.g., psychologists, social workers, marriage and family therapists), who have received specialized training in Collaborative Divorce and the Collaborative Practice; divorce coaching is not legal advice and is not therapy; it is not about placing blame, finding fault, or dealing with the past.

**Divorce Decree**: A court's formal order granting a termination of marriage; if a divorce case goes to trial and the judge issues a judgment, the judgment is confirmed when the decree is signed by the judge.

**Divorce Litigation**: A legal term meaning "carrying out a lawsuit"; the word "litigation" comes from the Latin word "litigatus" meaning "to dispute, quarrel, strive."

**Divorce Order**: Final order made by a court in a divorce case.

**Family Law**: An area of the law that deals with family-related issues and domestic relations, including:

- Marriage, civil unions, and domestic partnerships

- Issues that arise during marriage, including spousal abuse, adoption, child abuse, legitimacy, etc.

- The termination of the relationship and related matters including divorce, annulment, property settlements, alimony, custody, support, and parenting agreements

**Financial Counselor**: A professional who acts as a neutral party to help both spouses in gathering all the financial information about the couple or family in a supportive and nurturing environment; each client is encouraged to assist in financial disclosure and documentation of income, expenses, assets, and debts of the family; the essential shift is from a data focus to a system focus, whereby the financial counselor listens and then helps the clients understand the overall picture created by their particular family's financial situation; the knowledge gained by the clients through the data collection and documentation can aid each partner in achieving the financial settlement he or she desires.

**Four-Way Meeting(s)**: The Collaborative Process is conducted through a series of four-way meetings with both parties and their Collaborative attorneys; the sessions are intended to produce an honest exchange of information and expression of needs and expectations; mutual problem-solving by all the parties leads to the final divorce or marital settlement agreement; when additional professionals are added to the Collaborative Team, these sessions may become five-way or six-way meetings.

**Guardian ad litem**: Guardian ad litems are often appointed in divorce cases or in parenting time disputes to represent the interests of the minor children; the people appointed by the court as guardian ad litem varies by state, ranging from volunteers to social workers to attorneys; the guardian ad litem's only job is to represent the minor children's best interests.

**Interest-Based Negotiation**: Also called "interest-based bargaining" and "win-win bargaining," this is a negotiation strategy in which parties collaborate to find a "win-win" solution to their dispute; this strategy focuses on developing mutually beneficial agreements based on the interests of the parties; interests include the needs, desires, concerns, and fears important to each side; interest-based negotiation is important because it usually produces more satisfactory outcomes for the parties involved than does positional bargaining.

**Joint Custody**: Parents who don't live together have joint custody (also called shared custody) when they share the decision-making responsibilities for and/or physical custody and control, of their children; joint custody can be:

- Joint legal custody

- Joint physical custody, or

- Joint legal and physical custody

**Legal Custody**: Refers to the right as a parent to make important decisions about a child's health, well-being and education; a parent with legal custody can make decisions about schooling, religion, and medical care; most states regularly award joint legal custody, which means that the decision making is shared by both parents.

**Marital Settlement Agreement**: A written document that outlines the divorcing spouses' rights and agreements regarding property, support, and children; the issues that must be resolved and set forth in the agreement include:

- Division of assets and other property

- Repayment of debt and monies owed to creditors

- Alimony, child support, custody

**Mediation**: A method of resolving disputes in which a trained, neutral person (the mediator) helps the parties work out the solution for themselves. The mediator cannot give either party legal advice or be an advocate for either side. When an agreement is reached, the mediator may prepare a draft of the agreement for both sides to review with their lawyers.

**Mediator**: A neutral, impartial person who is trained in negotiation, conflict resolution, and communication skills. The mediator does not represent either party or take sides, but explains the mediation process to the parties and assists them to clarify issues, concerns, interests, needs, and values. The mediator may bring in and work with various other professionals as needed.

**No Fault Divorce**: "No fault" divorce describes any divorce where the spouse filing for the divorce does not have to prove that the other spouse did something wrong. All states allow no fault divorces. In some states the parties can just declare that they cannot get along ("irreconcilable differences" or "irremediable breakdown of the marriage"), and in others, they must live apart for a certain period of time in order to obtain a no fault divorce.

**Physical Custody**: Refers to the right as a parent to have a child living in his or her home; this arrangement can be joint physical custody to both parents, which is when the child(ren) spend significant time with both parents, or it can be a primary physical custody arrangement when the child(ren) live primarily at one parent's home with visitation to the other parent.

**Positional Bargaining**: This type of negotiating is based on fixed, opposing viewpoints (positions) and tends to result in compromise or not agreement at all (known as "impasse"). Often compromises do not efficiently satisfy the true interests of the parties, and instead, split the difference between the two positions, giving each person half of what he or she wants. Creative and integrative solutions achieved through interest-based negotiation, on the other hand, can potentially give both parties all of what they want.

**Prenuptial Agreement**: Also called a "premarital agreement," this legal document sets forth how property and debt will be split should the parties decide to divorce in the future.

**Separation**: When marriage partners sever their relationship with the intent of ending the marriage; separation does not have much legal effect in and of itself.

**Sole Custody**: One parent can have either sole legal custody or sole physical custody of a child, or both. Courts will generally award this to one parent if the other parent is deemed to be unfit, i.e., because of alcohol or drug dependency, a new partner who is unfit, or charges of child abuse or neglect. In most states, however, courts are moving away from awarding sole custody to one parent and toward enlarging the role that both parents play in the children's lives. Even if one parent is awarded sole (primary) physical custody, the parties still often share joint legal custody and the noncustodial parent has visitation. In that situation, the parents would make joint decisions about the child's upbringing, but one parent would be the primary physical caretaker, with the other parent having regular visitation.

**Spousal Support**: Also called "alimony" and "spousal maintenance," this term refers to monies paid by one spouse to the other to help the lesser-earning spouse maintain a certain standard of living. This is most common in situations where one spouse makes considerably more than the other.

**Uncontested Divorce**: One in which all issues have been agreed upon by the parties, and they reduce their agreement to writing and present it to the court; this can be achieved by the parties working with mediators and collaborative lawyers, as well as lawyers working in the traditional context. The vast majority of divorces cases are settled by agreement, but what occurs in the course of litigation and preparing for litigation can be damaging to the family relationships and resources.

**Zealous Advocacy**: In the zealous advocacy model, lawyers are taught to argue for the best result they can get for a client, regardless of how it effects or damages others. The adversarial system is thought of as an "engine" for discovering the truth. In theory, if each adversarial attorney pushes as hard as he can for his client, the truth will rise from the fray and justice will prevail. This may be necessary and work in criminal law cases, but in family law cases, zealous advocacy can escalate hostilities and the family can be injured as a result.

# ABOUT GRACEFUL DIVORCE SOLUTIONS

When I founded Graceful Divorce Solutions and launched my first website with that name, I was way out of my comfort zone. I was sure my friends and colleagues would laugh at that name, and some did. Using the words "graceful" and "divorce" in the same breath was a stretch for many people, especially lawyers.

But I wasn't writing for lawyers. I was writing for the hundreds of clients I have seen over the years who are looking for better ways to resolve the complicated and emotional issues involved in ending a marriage, ways the legal system just didn't accommodate. And the name I chose, Graceful Divorce Solutions, describes exactly the message I intended to send, so I didn't let the naysayers sway me.

Since launching that website in 2007, the feedback I've received has been astounding. What I have found is that people want reliable, trustworthy, information so they can understand their choices. They want to take an active role in resolving their differences. They want to resolve their differences as peacefully as possible and with integrity. If they have children, they want to protect them as much as possible. And with the current economy, they need to do all of this as economically as possible.

My goal with Graceful Divorce Solutions—whether it's the basic information at my website, specific articles on my Blog, or this book—is to provide valuable information and success strategies to help people through this process better. It's never easy to go through a divorce, but it doesn't have to be a bloodbath either. My goal is to start a movement, to provide a service, and to help implement change. There is no reason or excuse for the way many divorces go these days, and Graceful Divorce Solutions is designed to be a voice for the critical changes that are needed.

For more information about M. Marcy Jones and divorce options, please visit www.MMarcyJones.com. My services include speaking, coaching, and consulting, as well as representing clients in mediation, collaborative practice, and settlement negotiations.

For current articles and information about my speaking, writing and seminars, please visit my Blog at www.

GracefulDivorceSolutions.com. Sign up for the Free Report on The Four Divorces. And if there is a question or issue you're facing, you'll find a place there for submitting your questions or comments.

My final request is that you share this information with the next person. We all know people who are thinking about divorcing or going through divorce. Knowledge is power. Send them to my website or give them a copy of this book. It will help them and make a difference.

For a 30-minute, complementary consultation, please visit:

www.MMarcyJones.com

www.GracefulDivorceSolutions.com

# ABOUT THE AUTHOR

M. Marcy Jones is an author, speaker, lawyer, coach, and advocate for change. She went to Washington and Lee University School of Law after her own divorce and with two young children at home. Since graduating in 1995, she has worked as a prosecutor of domestic violence and sexual assault cases and then in private practice. Marcy is a settlement expert and a conflict resolution advocate.

Her passion and mission is to be an instrument of change in the way people divorce, in the legal system, and in the way lawyers represent clients in divorce. Like many lawyers in this practice area, she had reached a point where she was sadly disillusioned and seriously considered leaving the law. The traditional adversarial way of handling cases just didn't make sense when it came to ending marriages and making decisions about children. It became crystal clear to Marcy, from both her personal and professional experience with divorce, that the system was broken and change was needed.

Rather than leaving, though, she decided to take a stand by writing this book and encouraging change. Her mission is to provide honest, reliable information to people so they can make better and more informed choices for themselves, and to provide this information in a clear, concise, and readable format. In the often contentious field of family law, Marcy has adopted a very holistic approach to the process of divorce. Because a family is still a family, even after divorce, she advocates a win-win approach as the best way a family can navigate the process and retain positive relationships.

Marcy has had extensive training in mediation, negotiation, and collaborative practice. She is a member of the Virginia State Bar, Family Law Section, the Lynchburg Bar Association, the International Association of Collaborative Professionals, the Council for the Virginia Association of Collaborative Professionals, and is Vice-President of the Virginia Collaborative Professionals of Lynchburg. She has been instrumental in encouraging the use of the collaborative process in resolving divorce cases. She is also a certified personal coach, having received her certification through Coach Training Alliance in 2007.

With a passion for teaching others about effective communication and conflict resolution, Marcy constantly builds upon her strengths with additional trainings in collaborative law team effectiveness, mediation skills for collaborative attorneys, and interest-based negotiation. Through clear communication, peaceful resolution, and creative problem solving, she helps her clients navigate the legal process with integrity, dignity, and grace.

For comprehensive information and success strategies about divorce, visit www.GracefulDivorceSolutions.com and sign up to receive a Free Report now.

To learn more about Marcy or to book her to speak at your next event, go to her website at www.MMarcyJones.com.